Motown Murders and Ministry

By Jack Loshaw

Jack,
Hope you enjoy!

Jack Loshaw

ISBN 978-0-9826533-5-7
Second edition: December 2010
Printed in the United States of America

Oaklight Publishing
4306 Independence Street
Rockville, MD 20853
USA
http://oaklightpublishing.com

Dedication

I want to dedicate this book to my wife, Patricia, our three sons, Paul, Richard, and Ben, and our daughter, Kathy. My family was with me during my career as a detective, but I was never too comfortable sharing with them the things that took place. Now, that they are adults, I want to share with them my experiences and views of those happenings.

I also want to thank Traci Wardrop and Wendy Halsey for their help in editing the book. And thanks again to Terry Tracy for the artwork on the cover.

I went to the Homicide Unit in 1974 and two and a half years later my life was forever changed. I had an encounter with the Lord, what many would call a "born-again" experience. I had concerns that I would be ineffective as a detective if I were to relinquish control of my life to Him. I was in for a wonderful surprise.

Psalms 91:14-15 says, "For the Lord says, 'Because he loves Me, I will rescue him; I will make him great because he trusts in My name. When he calls on Me I will answer; I will be with him in trouble, and rescue him and honor him."

It seems to me that the Lord has gone out of His way to make me look good. For that I am grateful. I hope, as you read my words, that you will understand what makes me tick, and realize how He directs our steps.

Contents

Author's Note

Author's Note

I have written this book to show a segment of my life beginning at age twenty-four to when I joined the Detroit Police Department. It was also a time when the Viet Nam war was in full bloom. Many of the brightest young people were becoming disillusioned with leadership and there seemed to be a widening gulf of distrust between the generations.

I was a young married man, idealistic and enthusiastic, with great hopes for the future. I believed I could make a difference and was determined to do so. I had been married for four years and had a three-year-old son.

The stories I have written are all true. Although my memory is sharp, I do not pretend that many of the conversations are exact. They do reflect, however, the truth and tone of each one.

In many ways, this book is an adventure story, and indeed, a story of love . . . a love of fairness as I perceived it. I was promoted early in my career and in 1974, through some curious events I became a homicide detective. It was that same sad year that Detroit won the dubious honor of being crowned "The Murder Capital of America."

This book is about caring for victims and facing giants: whether they were disguised as defense lawyers in three-piece suites, street thugs armed with "Saturday night specials," or Quixote's windmills. I found pleasure in fighting the battle and had passion for my work as well as a deep concern for the city of Detroit.

This book was not written to bring people into my Christian belief. It was written to allow you to become aware of the down and dirty aspects of murder investigations. Along the way, my life changed as I found a relationship with God. Becoming a "real" Christian and continuing in police work was a true challenge. "East is east and west is west and never the twain shall meet" is often quoted in history classes and I felt much the same regarding the conflict of being a Christian and a homicide detective. In time, I came to realize that God would be with me regardless of my career path. As I slowly surrendered to Him, I began to experience the abundance of life and His effect upon the career I had chosen.

I was greatly troubled seeing many folks whose lives seemed hopeless and lacked any perceived abundance. From a police standpoint, I was determined to bring about what fairness I could and to do my part to alleviate some of the burdens brought by despair.

The Lord showed Himself to be faithful in that He not only approved of me and my profession, but brought honor and fulfillment to me.

I retired from the police department after seventeen and a half years, went to work at a car dealership for twelve years, and I am now, and have been for over fourteen years, an ordained minister at Mt. Zion Church in Clarkston, Michigan.

So, please read on as I present the stories of murder, the Motor City, and ministry.

Chapter One: The Detroit Police Department

I became a police officer quite by accident. It was in the summer of 1967, I was twenty-four years old, married, the father of a three-year-old son, and had a steady job. My best friend, Mike Durecki, and I had worked together at two other jobs and he was unemployed at the time. He had filled out an application to join the Detroit Police Department and seemed nervous about it. Applying was the first and easiest step in the process. The big test, as he explained, was the physical aspect—a strength and endurance test that was being held on the upcoming Saturday. He needed moral support and convinced me to go with him, stating that applications would be on hand.

"It's just a matter of doing some pushups, climbing a rope, stuff like that. Come with me, it'll be fun and the worst that can happen is we wind up looking like the guy who got the beach sand kicked in his face. And if that doesn't work we can join the circus or become firemen or something."

Mike was hardly persuasive but the thought of participating in a Junior Olympics was intriguing. I asked Mike if his wife was threatening to divorce him and he said, "No, it's worse than that . . . she's threatening to kill me."

He was some smooth talker and with his wife putting pressure on him to get a job, any kind of job, I knew he would like an escort to go with him. So, when Saturday arrived I went along for the fun of it.

We drove to the recruiting area and, to my surprise, there were over three hundred applicants milling around. Real police officers appeared wearing their Sam Brown belts and menacing looking revolvers hanging in holsters on their hips. They broke us up into groups of twenty or so and we started doing manly things.

We were young and most were strutting and pacing around like bulls with smoke coming out of their nostrils. The smell of testosterone filled the air. I looked around and it seemed like they all had muscles bigger than mine; a few even had tattoos. The thought crossed my mind, "what the heck am I doing here?"

We competed in nine or ten events: the standing broad jump, 100-yard dash, one-mile run, climbing a rope, pushups, chin-ups, and other exercises. Mike and I were competing well against the other guys and finished near the top of our groups.

I noticed that after four or five events many of the applicants disappeared. And, somehow, I had managed to impress the recruiter. He told me to get on the weight scale and I tipped it at a solid 142 pounds. A frown crossed the sergeant's face as he said, "You're a little light in the fanny, son. The minimum weight for your height is 156. We're gonna have to put some meat on your skinny frame."

Now, I'm sure that the sergeant had earned a degree in dietary science because his next words were, "Now, listen to me. You gotta put on at least seven pounds to even get in the academy and you gotta do it in two weeks. So here's what you do. You go home and start eatin' lots of bananas, and lots of spaghetti and lots of potatoes—things like that 'cause that's how you gain weight. And in two Saturdays from now you get your butt down here, and by the way don't even take a bowel movement that morning, ya hear, 'cause you gotta put on the seven pounds."

I thought to myself, "It's taken me twenty-four years to get to 142 and now he wants me to add seven pounds in two weeks. Ain't no way."

So I went home and told my wife how well I had done. She rolled her eyes when I told her about the weight problem and said she would try to help me. I could tell she wasn't impressed with the recruiter's plan of attack.

The two weeks raced by and I became introspective. "There's no way I can gain seven pounds in two weeks." And then I wondered, *would I make it as a cop, how long would it take me before I got myself killed?* These seemed like sensible questions at the time.

On that fateful Saturday, Mike responded. I reported to the sergeant's office at the academy. The door was open and the three-striper was seated at his desk. It was a sparsely decorated room with two hardback chairs, a beaten wooden desk, a calendar with a partially clad woman decorating it, a typewriter with no paper, and the sergeant.

"Come on in. You ready to jump on the scale?"

I looked around and wondered where the scale was. "Yes, sir, 'bout as ready as I can be."

He walked over to a bathroom door and against the wall was a height and weight scale. He told me to get on. He measured me at five feet eleven and one half inch (somehow I was a half inch shorter than when measured two weeks earlier). He moved the metal weight in the area of 150. Before the needle could stop bouncing he pushed back the weight measure and said, "Nice job! Seven pounds exactly! We'll put the other seven on when you get to the academy. You know, the shorter you are the less you have to weigh."

He went on to tell me that an investigator would come out to my home. "Make sure you don't have any alcohol in the house and tell your wife to make sure the place is clean. Investigators are just looking for reasons to rule you out. And he will also talk to your neighbors so if you've had words with any, do your best to make up with them before he gets there."

"And once that part is completed you will have to face a three member board who will question you about street situations."

He congratulated me and told me I would make a good cop. He and I shook hands and for the first time in my life, I began to imagine myself as a Detroit Police Officer.

On the way home, I told Mike what the sergeant had said. "He told me that Pat and I should make sure there were no dust webs in the house or they could fail me. I'm not sure I want some guy snooping through my place. What have you gotten me into? And then he said there would be three cops who are going to question me about 'street situations.' I can only imagine what that's going to be like."

Mike responded, "Oh, don't worry about it. We'll get through this and it's gonna be fun."

A few days later, an investigator went to Mike's home, checked things over, and interviewed a few neighbors. The recruiting sergeant phoned Mike and told him he had passed and they would set up his personal interview in a few days.

A day later, the same investigator arrived at our home just after 6 p.m. It had been a week since I had been weighed. He was a tall imposing man who looked older than my father. He was unsmiling, mean looking, and I could see the butt end of his gun tucked in his beltline. He eyes were piercing and it seemed to me that he was very intent on finding something wrong with our home. He looked in the refrigerator, under the beds, walked through the backyard (I assumed he was looking for weeds), and as I walked with him he looked at my skinny frame and said, "What kind of a cook is your wife?"

"She's pretty good."

He continued looking me over, from top to bottom, and I pictured him thinking that I had been underfed. He put his hand in his pocket and the butt end of his pistol stuck out above his belt. He said, "So, you want to be a cop, eh? What's that about?"

I wanted to tell him that I only applied because my cowardly friend, Mike, was too afraid to go by himself, but I lied and said instead, "It's something I've always wanted to be."

With that, he smirked, shook my hand, wished my wife well, and left.

Two days later the sergeant called and told me I had passed the investigation. He notified me that I would be called back to the academy for the final step in becoming a police officer. The oral interview would be conducted by the three-member board and was set for Tuesday, July 25, 1967.

Then, on July 23, at 12th Street and Clairmount, the Detroit Police Department raided an after-hours drinking establishment. In a relatively short time, a riot broke out that continued for five days. The governor of Michigan, George Romney, ordered the Michigan State Police into Detroit and President Lyndon Johnson sent in U.S. Army troops. All active Detroit Police Officers were ordered into service, with leave days and vacations cancelled.

Weeks later the news media in Detroit reported that forty-three people had been killed, 467 injured, over 2,000 buildings burned down, and more than 7,200 people arrested.

Late Monday night on July 24th, the recruiting sergeant called me at home. "Do you see what's happening to Detroit? Do you still want to be a cop?"

"Yes, I do."

He paused for a moment and said, "Well, as you can imagine, your interview has been delayed. I don't know when we will get Detroit straightened out, but if we do, or when we do, I will call you with a new date for your interview."

"I understand."

The sergeant paused for a minute and uttered, "Yeah, well, you better make sure your wife is in agreement with you, because it's a bad time to be a police officer."
My wife, Pat, and I talked things over. It was a terrible thing to see our city going up in flames. It hurt everybody and fear had spread throughout the city. I felt firm in my desire to go into law enforcement, and Pat told me that I had her support.

Once the riot ended, I was notified to report to the Detroit Police Academy. On August 14, 1967, Mike picked me up, we enrolled, and were officially named as probationary patrolmen. The academy sessions only lasted eight weeks, after which I was sent to my first assignment, the 5th Precinct.

Chapter Two: Trouble, Trouble, Trouble

In the old days before EMS, 911, VCRs, DVDs, the Internet, and cable TV, the Detroit Police Department was responsible for notifying the next of kin whenever there was an unnatural death. Today, this is handled by people trained to deliver the bad news.

In May of 1968, I was assigned to work a scout car as the junior partner of a cagey old veteran named Tony Piccono. He had twenty-two years of experience, all of it at the 5th precinct. He didn't expect to be promoted and hoped to retire in three years to collect his city pension. He had two grown children who never talked to him and was married to his fourth wife. That marriage was on shaky grounds.

Tony was an unlikely looking police officer. He was short and portly and his belly overlapped his belt. He had just passed his fiftieth birthday and his hair was as black as the first day he joined the department. Most cops suspected that he dyed his braids, but he strongly denied it. He smiled often and whistled constantly. As a matter of fact, he was an unlikely acting police officer, too. He always seemed upbeat and enjoyed working with the younger officers. The street hadn't taken its toll upon his spirit, although his body had paid the price for years of rotating shifts and chowing down on Coney Island hot dogs at four in the morning. Tony was a pleasant man to work with and didn't take himself or the job too seriously. He was proud to be a cop, so much so that he had his badge tattooed on his right bicep. It was something that caused a lot of ribbing.

"Tony, with that stupid tattoo on your arm, is it any wonder that you never worked undercover?"

"Well, for all you know, maybe I never wanted to work in plain clothes, plus I like to know what I'm going to wear each day and putting on this uniform makes my choices easy."

He would then flash his big smile and whistle some unknown tune.

Tony was a nice guy, good natured, and easy going, but had one small flaw. He had a problem with alcohol and couldn't wait for his shift to end so that he could relax with a twelve pack. He often said, "Drinking isn't my problem, staying sober is."

It seemed to me that he had been traumatized by a certain *rite of passage*: the fiftieth birthday. It dawned on him that life was passing him by. He also suffered from an innate fear of his ex-wives dragging him back into court and requesting more alimony, hoping to latch on to his soon-arriving department pension.

We began work that day at 7:45 a.m. It was a bright Sunday morning. The police radio gave us our first assignment, "Scout 5-1, call dispatch." That sort of message usually indicated something of a sensitive nature that the dispatchers didn't want spoken over the airwaves, such as "can you guys bring us some donuts?" We went to a call box located in the adjoining precinct, the 7th, one I didn't know existed, and Tony jumped out, smiling as usual. He opened the box and with his back to me talked on the phone. When he ambled back to the car, I could smell the faint odor of alcohol and it dawned on me that Tony might have sipped something from within "his" call box. He tried to conceal that he was taking a quick nip, but didn't hide his effort too well when some of the liquid missed its mark and dropped onto his uniform shirt. Oh, well, such was life and Tony was happy.

Back in the car, with eyes sparkling, he said, "Dispatch said that some nice old fellow named Willie Tyner and a friend had gone fishing early this morning out in New Baltimore." In his eagerness to get fishing, Willie had somehow managed to get himself killed by stepping out into oncoming traffic on Jefferson Avenue and was run over by a car. "We've been ordered to his last known address of 5221 Hurlbut to notify his family."

We drove over to the house and parked in front of the two-story frame dwelling. There was more dirt on the lawn than grass. The home was in dire need of paint and the sun had baked most of it down to the bare wood.

Even though I was riding shotgun and responsible for writing all the reports, I knew that in a sensitive situation like this, Tony would do the talking. He was seasoned and would know what to say.

I knocked on the frame of the screen door that led to the upper flat. The screen was bowed out and there were gaps where the screen had once been attached. As I knocked, the door rebounded against my knuckles. Two knocks gave you four, three gave you six. It was kind of fun knocking on that door. If this was indeed Mr. Tyner's house, it was clear to me that he must have been a better fisherman than a repairman.

A frail little dark-skinned girl came down the stairs. She was five or six years old and was wearing a summer dress that was much too short. Her hair was shooting up in all angles from her head and it was obvious that no one had bothered to comb it. When she saw us, her eyes became bigger than saucers. She turned and yelled upstairs, "Mama, mama, it's the po-leece, it's the po-leece."

From upstairs we could hear the sounds of heavy footsteps. They sounded like those of a large woman and we could hear her talking, "What's this man done now? Trouble, trouble, all that man does is bring me trouble! That man just keeps bringin' trouble my way! He ain't never been nothin' but trouble!"

As she trudged down the stairs she was shaking her head and saying over and over,

"Oh, my, more trouble, more trouble!"

We saw that she was indeed a large lady who was wearing oversized slippers which flapped against her heels with every step. She was wrapped in an old chenille robe missing half of its fuzz and the belt of her robe was straining to keep her covered. It appeared that she and her daughter shared the same hair stylist. When she finally arrived at the door she said, "What's that man done now?"

Tony looked her dead in the eyes and said, "Ma'am your troubles are over!"

Chapter Three: Angel Unaware

As I have said before, 1967 was not a good year to join the police department. Terrible riots had taken place in many of the large cities across America and Detroit was the site of one of the worst riots in our country's history. In less than a week, hundreds of businesses, homes and cars were set on fire. People were killed, hundreds hurt, thousands arrested and property values in the millions were lost. Race relations were in shambles and police-community relations were below zero. I was smart enough to join the department immediately after the riot, and began training in August.

The police department was under great pressure to get more police officers out on the street. After six weeks of training at the academy, I was sent to the 5th Precinct at Jefferson and St. Jean, on the east side. It was anything but a garden spot. It seemed that everyone hated us. The term "pigs" was becoming common when referring to us. There were many black people who were vocal in their distrust and dislike for police officers. There was racial tension between blacks and whites and many of the poorer white folks appeared to trust police officers about as much as they trusted black people. The riot had brought out the worst in people and it was a racially charged time. There was a smattering of older white and black people who couldn't afford to move out and many lived in fear. So upon entering the 5th, I quickly learned that the working officers felt it was an "us, against them" kind of thing. It was the old story: "they weren't paranoid, everyone really was against them."

Many of the veteran officers retired after the riot. Dozens of police officers sought and found jobs in the suburban communities. Many others quit in disgust, thinking of better ways to earn an income. What was left behind was a disgruntled group of veterans and a growing group of young, inexperienced officers.

Among the young officers that I became friends with were many members of the precinct softball team. One of the nicest guys on the team was a twenty-three-year-old veteran of nine months, named Paul Bentley. He made the team, not because of his athleticism (which was minimal), but because of his ability to get along with everyone. He was the slowest man on the team, thus earning the right to be called "Bentfoot." He had the lowest batting average, the weakest and most inaccurate arm, and his glove was made of wrought iron. Other than those deficiencies, it was nice having him on the team. His lovely wife, Kathy, and their little boy faithfully attended every game.

We played the games in the mornings. On a beautiful July day, we lost a heartbreaker by the score of 23 to 5, and Paul had contributed heavily to the cause by bouncing into two double plays. The team rallied around him with encouraging words like, "Paul, you're the slowest guy ever to play baseball," and "man, you really do stink." Paul remained undaunted, thinking they were only kidding. He had a terrific innocent quality that made everyone like him. Plus, he sounded like a kid. When boys reach puberty, their voices drop an octave or two. Not Paul though; his voice remained at tenor pitch. At the ripe age of twenty-three, he sounded like an eleven year old.

Paul had great enthusiasm for police work. He worked very hard, he tried very hard, and he cared very much. He was determined to become good at it. He was such an innocent kid that I think it must have been extremely difficult for him to try to develop street smarts. He seemed shocked by violence and cruelty and was constantly in awe of criminal behavior.

In October of 1969, Paul was assigned to work with another young officer by the name of Bill Sandall. Bill was not nearly as innocent as Paul, but just as inexperienced. I was working with a one-year veteran named Ben Lawrence. Ben had the same boyish innocence of Paul. Ben was born and raised in Grayling, Michigan, and was totally overwhelmed by the streets and the people of Detroit. He was well liked by the other officers, who hung the nickname "Opie" on him. He was a lousy ballplayer, too.

On that same October evening, at 11:20 p.m., Ben and I stopped at a restaurant to finish off a report. While sipping a coffee, I heard Paul Bentley's high-pitched voice over the prep radio. He and Sandall were in hot pursuit of a car occupied by two people. We ran to our car and headed in the direction of the chase. Paul was screaming unintelligibly into the radio, but we were able to determine that the chased car had cracked up. We turned the corner of Charlevoix and Belvidere, and saw the blue flashing lights of their car. The car they were chasing had plowed into a telephone pole and looked disabled. We saw Bentley walking from between the houses with a man in custody, hands handcuffed behind his back.

Bentley yelled at me, "Jack! You're always messin' with me about how slow I am. Well, I want you to know that I caught this guy all by myself."

"Yeah, well, what did you do with the guy's crutches?" I retorted.

"Funny, very funny."

There was a woman sitting in the passenger seat of the disabled car who had made no attempt to flee.

At that time, Lieutenant Ross Jackson and Sergeant Stanley Wrobel drove up. Officer Sandall reported to them that they had tried to stop the car for a moving violation. The car sped on and a quick chase had gone on for about a mile until the car turned on Belvidere and struck the phone pole. The driver's door had buckled a bit, so the driver crawled over the female passenger and exited through her door. The female remained seated. Bentley gave chase on foot and captured the man. We ran the plate and the VIN and were informed by radio that the car was not stolen. The prisoner admitted to not having a driver's license and that was the reason for fleeing. The lieutenant told us that there was no reason to impound the car and to leave the scene and get back "in service." He told us that Bentley and Sandall would take the prisoner and the female into the precinct, which was only six blocks away. We drove off.

Within one minute, I was driving east on Kercheval. As we approached Hart street, I heard Sandall's voice screaming over the radio. I couldn't make out a word of what was said but I knew that something was very wrong. I made a U-turn and headed back to the scene. As I turned onto St. Jean, I saw their police car parked under a streetlight. The engine was running and the car was in the parked position. Paul was in the front passenger's seat. The driver's door was open, as were the two rear doors. Sandall was walking around in circles in the middle of St. Jean. I could see that he had blood dripping from his left ear and the back of his head. His blue shirt was covered with blood. I jumped out of my car and ran to him. He sat down in the middle of the street. I looked into his car and there was Bentley. Paul was slumped forward in the front passenger seat, clipboard on his lap, a pencil in his hand—about to make the last entry on his activity sheet. The contents of the activity sheet would be forever unreadable. They were saturated with Paul's blood. He had been shot, no, executed, by a gunshot to the back of his head. My slow-footed, innocent friend was dead and my heart was broken.

Police cars came from everywhere in the city. Even though we all knew he was dead, a crew of officers pulled Bentley out of the car and raced him down to Detroit General Hospital. Then another crew threw Sandall into the back seat of a police car and conveyed him to the hospital too. He had also been shot in the back of the head. Fortunately, the bullet hit the mastoid section of his head, followed a track under the scalp, and exited through the "hangy-down" part of his ear. He told me, later, that it felt like he had been hit in the head with a sledgehammer.

A massive manhunt went into action. The fugitives were described as a black male, tentatively identified as Horace Watson, thirty-five years old, 5'10", and 165 pounds. The other fugitive was a black female, first name of Justine, about twenty-five years old, heavy set, and believed to be the girlfriend of Watson. It was assumed that Watson was still handcuffed. Any other information would have to wait until Sandall was able to talk.

Ben Lawrence and I were ordered to the Homicide Bureau for our reports. It was also my task to inventory all of Bentley's personal effects. His bloodied clothing and personal items were taken from his body and sent over to Homicide. I found a corner and started going through his belongings and, when no one was looking, I cried. This was so unreal. Paul couldn't be dead. Why did the lieutenant order us back on patrol? We should have just followed their car into the station. How could this happen?

Sometime around 4 a.m., I was finished with my paperwork and made the one block walk over to Detroit General Hospital to see Bill Sandall. His head was wrapped with white gauze and tape. I told him he looked like a swami. I pulled up a chair and sat down next to his bed. He looked good, considering what he had been through, and even sounded good. He began to tell what had happened.

"Jack, it was really weird. We put the man in the back seat and he seemed like a decent enough guy. He even apologized for running. Then I went and got the woman and she seemed nice too. I told her that we were just driving her up to the station 'cause we didn't want to see her left out on the streets. She sat in the seat behind Paul. I turned on Charlevoix, went over the one block to St. Jean, and a block later I heard an explosion. I didn't know what was going on. Then I heard another explosion and I thought I'd been hit with a sledgehammer. About then, I realized that they were shootin' at us. I stopped the car and rolled out onto St. Jean. I must have been yelling into the prep but I'm not sure. Anyhow, the two of them got out of the car and started running down the street. Watson still had cuffs on, but I didn't see any gun. I started shooting at them, but I wasn't seeing them too good. Man, they got away. I don't believe it. They killed Paul, and I let them get away."

He began crying and before long my eyes were wet.

"Bill, it wasn't your fault. You took a head shot yourself. It's a wonder that you were able to do what you did. Don't blame yourself."

I took his hand and we both wiped tears away. He was all of twenty-four, and I was the old man at twenty-six. Our lives would never be the same.

"Jack, I know you're a religious guy and I gotta tell you, something really strange happened out there."

"What was that?"

"Well, you probable think I'm crazy, but after I had emptied my gun and I was just standing there thinking that I was dying too, this older black man came up to me and put his arm around me and said, "You're going to be alright, son, you're going to be alright.""

In my mind, I began to retrace what had happened. I knew from the time I heard Sandall's voice over the radio, until the time of our arrival, not more than twenty to thirty seconds could have passed. I didn't see any older black man anywhere.

"Bill, I sure didn't see him."

"Yeah, I know. Jack, I swear, he just kinda vanished, know what I mean? Or maybe I imagined it."

Bill tried to sit up but fell back across the pillow. He said, "Do you think he was an angel?"

"Well, it wouldn't surprise me. I've heard that angels are sometimes sent as messengers and right about that time I'm sure you needed some encouragement. One thing is for sure, you should have been killed tonight, so I believe there's a lot you will accomplish in your life. When you get out of here we will sit down and talk all of this over."

We shook hands and I drove back to the precinct, dropped off the scout car and reported to the lieutenant. He came from behind the desk and shook my hand.

"Jack, you've been involved in one of the worst things a cop can go through. You keep your chin up and you'll get through this. We all are hurt by this, but we'll get through. Go home and get some sleep, kiss your wife and son, and we'll see you back here tomorrow."

I drove home and had never felt so lonely in my life.

As I got into bed Pat asked me if everything was alright and I told her that things were good and I would talk to her in the morning about what had happened. I was exhausted and in a few minutes I went into a deep sleep.

The investigators learned that Watson had gone to friends and relatives who refused to help him. He and Justine were afraid they would be shot by police officers, so they turned themselves in to a priest at an eastside Catholic Church. When Watson walked into the sanctuary he was *still* wearing the handcuffs. His girlfriend, Justine Thomas, was still with him. In his statement to the Homicide detectives, Watson admitted to carrying the gun that night but when he had crawled over Justine and passed her the gun. She tucked it into her waistband and when the scout car entered St. Jean Street, she shot both officers.

At the trial, the jury somehow reached a verdict finding her guilty of second-degree murder because the prosecutor had failed to prove premeditation. The judge decided that a sentence of twenty to thirty years was fair. By the time she was released, Paul's little boy had reached his twenty-second birthday and his wife, Kathy, was still a widow.

Chapter Four: The Trip to Homicide

So You Want To Be A Homicide Detective?

As I have mentioned before, I graduated from the Detroit Police Academy in October of 1967 and was assigned to the uniform division of the 5th Precinct. It was located on the east side of Detroit and bordered on the Detroit River. It was a great place to learn about police activity and offered a wide-ranging view of Detroit. To say the least, it was a diverse area. In the precinct was the Manoogian Mansion, where the mayor lived; a very wealthy section called Indian Village, where many of the "old money" folks resided; a small section called the "Appalachian District" which many impoverished white people called home; a very large area with a growing contingent of black people lived; and a smaller area where middle-class white folks had mail boxes that bordered the wealthy suburban community of Grosse Pointe. From a racial standpoint, African Americans outnumbered Caucasians by quite a large margin.

I worked in the 5th for three years, and during that time came under the supervision of Lieutenant Stan Langeman. He was my shift boss for two years. He transferred to become the officer in charge of a newly created unit named the Community Relations Section. He had a couple of his men, who had previously worked at the 5th, approach me and suggested that I transfer to that unit and I did. There were many perks for transferring to that unit, the prime one being no midnight shifts.

I was there for a year and a half and worked to set up programs to facilitate neighboring community groups working with police officers. Neighborhood watch programs were organized and much of my time was spent directing them in crime prevention areas and going to various high schools to work with administrators, teachers, and students. Although it was enjoyable, I missed the real police work of catching bad guys, so I transferred back to the 5th. The lieutenant and other officers from the Community Relations Section assumed I had lost my senses for leaving such a soft job. They believed that I deserved to be pushing a scout car around on the midnight shift, which I soon did. After a couple of weeks on the midnight watch, I questioned my sanity too.

Prior to transferring out of the Community Relations Section, it was announced that the sergeant's promotional examination would be held in June. I was told that any chance of me being promoted was slim because the test was weighted heavily for those with high seniority, armed service duties, and high service ratings. I had only four and a half years of service at that time and as an officer with limited experience, I was told that the test would be a good learning exercise. The supervisors told all of the young guys that, in time, the test would prove beneficial if you hoped to ever be promoted.

I studied a couple of hours a day preparing for the test and, to my surprise, scored highly. In September of 1972, I was rewarded with sergeant's stripes. The police commissioner, John Nichols, told everyone in attendance that I was the second youngest in seniority promoted to that rank. It was a bit embarrassing and was certainly news to me.

After a couple of weeks of sergeants training at the Detroit Police Academy, I was assigned to the uniformed division of the 7th Precinct. All of us in the Sergeant's School were informed that we would be on a one-year probationary period and any negative feedback could cause the loss of our stripes.

The 7th was another east side precinct that bordered my former one. I worked with many older officers and, to my relief, found that they were willing to take advice and orders from me. While assigned there, I worked undercover with a group of men while we investigated areas like liquor, gambling, vice, narcotics activities, burglary surveillance, and other duties. It was during this time that I became familiar with preparing search warrants.

I was at the 7th precinct for one year and my last duty was investigating police officers accused of accepting bribes. A team from the Internal Affairs Section was sent to oversee the operation. I watched the way the men from that unit operated and decided, quite quickly, that I wanted nothing to do with them or their outfit. When the bribery case was completed and the officers were cleared, the Internal guys looked disappointed. I found it very disturbing that "regular officers" were looked down upon by those who were called upon to investigate them.

When that assignment was finished, I was called in to see my supervising lieutenant. He thanked me for my work and told me that the inspector from Internal Affairs had called and wanted me to transfer to his unit. I explained that I wasn't interested and he said, "You really aren't in a position to say no to those guys, Jack. They can help you advance in the department or can cause you a lot of grief."

"Boss, are you saying that by refusing, they can hurt me. Sounds a little like blackmail."

"Don't worry about what it's called. Don't refuse, just go there and do a good job."

"From what I've seen, there is no way I could work with those folks. I think I will have to take my chances. I don't like their haughty attitudes and the way they look down on street cops."

"I think you're making a big mistake, but I understand and can't argue with you. I wish you the best of luck, Jack."

It sounded like he was saying goodbye and, in the same breath, appreciated my decision.

The Court Section

On the next day, I reported to work and my lieutenant told me that the inspector wanted to see me. His only words to me were, "You've been assigned to the Court Section. I don't know whose soup you peed in, but that's where you work."

"The Court Section! Where's the Court Section?"

"It's downtown at 1300. Just go down there and any cop in the building will tell you where to go. You've got a long way to go before you retire so I advise you to become a little more adaptable."

I thought to myself, "adaptable." Now I've gotta learn to be adaptable.

I made it to the Court Section and soon realized that most of the men there had reached their twenty-fifth year retirement age or were quickly approaching it. It was the kind of job where a man could kick back and relax . . . a place many old-time sergeants would have killed to have been placed, but it certainly wasn't for a young crime-fighter like me. I had six years on the job and retirement was a distant glimmer.

The unit consisted of thirty-six sergeants who were responsible for "running" the warrant requests of the various precinct detectives to the prosecutor's office located in the Frank Murphy Hall of Justice. The request would then be approved or denied by an assistant prosecutor. If the warrant request was approved, the sergeant would then take it to the signing judge at the court where he would be sworn (under information and belief) and it would be signed. It seemed that we were nothing more than messenger boys and our services could have been used in much wiser ways. Detroit was a crime-ridden city and we were doing little to deter it.

Since becoming a police officer, I had hoped that I would be called to become a member of the Homicide Unit. I pictured homicide detectives as being the cream of the crop and working with them would have fulfilled my dreams. Working in the Court Section was not a stepping stone.

Four months into my time at the Court Section, I was in the office filing papers when the inspector from Homicide walked in. He was well known and he and I went to the same church. I knew about him, but he knew little about me.
"How do you like working here, Jack?"

"Well, inspector, it's a good place to work but kind of boring. Actually, I don't like what I'm doing at all. I feel like I'm just a paper shuffler."

I saw his eyes narrow and his facial expression showed displeasure. "Well, I think you might need to adjust your attitude some. The Court Section is important and you need to pour yourself into it. There's a lot you can learn from working with the prosecutors and judges, but you can't do it with a poor attitude. You need to work on it . . . learn how the system works and come see me in a few months and maybe we can talk about you coming to homicide."

There I was talking to the boss of homicide who told me that if I put my energy into what I was doing then I might get the call.

I told him that I would give it my best and he stuck out his hand for me to shake. His face brightened and he said very simply, "Keep on pluggin'."
One month later, everything changed. The inspector was transferred out of homicide and I knew I was buried in the Court Section. My chances of being called to homicide were remote.

Another month went by and I felt that I had reached my limit. It was a Friday in March of 1974 and I had just finished typing out stacks of subpoenas. I walked down the hall to the Homicide Unit and knocked on Inspector Ross Barnett's door. Barnett had worked his way through homicide as a sergeant, lieutenant, and had recently been promoted to the rank of inspector. He was a Korean War veteran and nearly sixty years old. He stood over 6'2" and weighed around 240 pounds. His face was reddish and he had a full head of thick gray hair. His voice was gruff and he spoke with authority. He knew what he was doing and had twenty-three years of experience to prove it. I had never talked to him before and I was nervous as I stood at his door. He called me in and said, "Who are you looking for?"

"I was hoping I could talk to you, sir. I was just wondering if you were accepting any transfers into your unit."

It was late in the afternoon and I knew he had better things to do. His eyes glanced back to the papers in front of him and I knew I was nothing but an interruption. "Go ahead, sit down. Who are you and how long have you been on the job?"

"Jack Loshaw and I have just over six and a half years."

He had a slight smirk on his face and said, "Six and a half years, eh? Don't you think you're a little green to even think of coming to homicide?"

"I know that's not a lot of time, but I believe I can do the job."

"Do you now. Where are you working?"

That was the question that I dreaded but knew was coming.

"I'm over at the Court Section."

His smirk grew wider and I could see he was studying my face. I tried not to look nervous.

"Did you transfer to the Court Section or tick someone off?"

I knew that any answer I came up with would sound stupid so I said, "I'm not sure, but I don't think I impressed Internal Affairs too much."

He smiled with that answer and said, "You could have done worse things. Have you made any arrests at the Court Section?"

"There aren't too many chances for arrests in that unit. I'm learning to deal with the prosecutors, judges, and courts. Just trying to learn what it's all about."

I wasn't happy with my answer and I knew he certainly was familiar with the courts. I felt I had failed the interview and my heart sank.

He folded his hands in front of him and asked, "Tell me, what makes you think that you have what it takes to be a homicide detective?"

"Well, I've done a good job on the street and I know I can handle the job."

"You do, huh? Well, right now I have all the men I need but I will keep you in mind."

I thanked him for his time and walked out with my tail between my legs. As I walked to my desk, I wondered how quickly my next eighteen and a half years would crawl by. I patted myself on the back for having the guts to knock on the boss's door and kicked myself for the lousy answers I'd given.

The following Monday, I went to my desk at the Court Section and was told that I had been transferred to the Homicide Unit. I was beginning to realize that dreams do come true.

I will now ask you to follow along as I relate a few of the cases that I was involved in during my nine years at the Homicide Unit.

Chapter Five: The William Brown Case

On March 22, 1978, a LEIN (Law Enforcement Information Network) message was sent from Dade County, Florida, to the Homicide Division of the Detroit Police Department. It said:

"On January 2, 1978, two of our male residents were shot to death by a man identified as William Brown. The subject is reportedly in the Detroit area. Fingerprints from the homicide scene have confirmed his identity. His identification number is 123757 and our warrant number is DC 223778. Please try to apprehend and if successful notify Sergeants Callebro and Muñoz."

I had finished my last case three days before and was looking into one of my old files when Inspector Ross Barnett walked over to me. He handed me the LEIN message and said, "Since you've got nothin' better to do than read about your old cases, why don't you try to accomplish something today? Maybe you can help out another department 'cause you sure ain't doin' nothin' around here." With those polite words of encouragement, he handed me the LEIN message and walked back to his office.

The message was clear and it seemed like an easy enough task, so I walked down to Identification Section and pulled the file on #123757. William Brown was described as a black male, twenty- six years old, 5'10", 145 pounds, and light complexion, with no facial hair except a wispy mustache. His arrest record was for small-time, two-bit stuff; nothing to indicate he was assaultive. There were several different addresses for him at his various times of arrest.

I took his identification number with me to the basement where Central Photo was located and had several mug shot photographs made. Once I had the photos and warrant number, I went back to Homicide and enlisted the help of my partner, Cal Noles. We went out to the streets to look for the Dade County killer.

We visited the various addresses where he had supposedly resided. One was a vacant field, another would have placed him in the middle of the Detroit River, and yet another was an abandoned house. At the only address still in existence, a very elderly couple stated that they had lived there for thirty-one years and had never known a William Brown. I showed them the mug shot and they admitted that he looked familiar, but, no, they did not know him.

From that point we drove around to a few of the hangouts of street people. Cal and I had a very good rapport with many of the prostitutes, Murphy men, snitches, Jakey bums, and even junkies from the street. Street people were always in need of favors and they were great sources of information, so I made it a point to always have a few on my side. I passed out several of Williams Brown's mugs and let everyone know that I would deeply appreciate their assistance in catching this guy. We left our cards and then drove off. We knew from past experience that whenever a street thug got into trouble we could expect a call with wonderful information, as long as we returned the favor.

One of the prostitutes, a girl named Georgia, used to call me about once a week. She liked the fact that I paid attention to her. From her viewpoint as an eighteen-year-old girl, I was an important person, with a high position, and it was nice knowing someone who wasn't out trying to get something from her. She insisted that whenever she called me we would use the alias "GA." Since she was the only GA I knew and likely the only one she knew, we shared a clever code name.

GA was some young lady. She had worked the streets for over two years, and knew just about every John and hoodlum that traveled Woodward Avenue. She was different from most of her competitors. Most street girls were far from being attractive, but GA was not only pretty but quite intelligent. She was also on the tall side, nearly 5'8", and slim. She bragged about wearing a size one. I would see her on her corner about once a week and most times she would try to ignore me, so we did our best work by phone. She must have had fifty pairs of shoes, most with heels four to six inches high. Wearing them propelled her over six feet tall. When she added her blond wig, she was the tallest of all the Woodward Avenue girls. GA was easy to spot and she liked it that way.

When I needed to see GA face to face, we would set up a meeting. To help cover her, I would put Ontario plates on my private car before meeting her. As far as I knew there were no other cops driving around with foreign plates and she could explain me to anyone as one of her regular Windsor, Canada, Johns.

Actually, I was just like so many of her customers—I was after something, too. It wasn't her body, though, but the information to which she had access. I told her that she was wasting her life and that she didn't belong on the streets. She laughed and told me that I was old fashioned, but in her heart I could tell that she liked me advising her.

"Now, you tell me Sgt. Jack, where can I make the money I make by doing anything legal?"

"You're only eighteen, how long do you think you can do what you do and still stay alive."

"Well, I only plan on doing this for a while, maybe five or six years, and then I will have enough money that maybe I will become a lawyer or something."

"Oh, I see. So you plan on getting your record expunged?"

"What? Is that a cop term? I don't think I want nothin' expunged!"

I could tell from her crooked smile that she knew exactly what expunged meant.

Before I left she hit me up for a pack of Kools that she knew I had stashed away for her. As I pulled them from the glove box, I told her, "You look more like a Virginia Slim package than you do Kools."

"Do any of you white folks smoke Kools, Sgt. Jack?"

"The only ones I know of are suffering from emphysema."

"See, all ya'all gotta be cute."

"Listen, GA, you know I love you."

She had an innocent smile, one she had before ever hitting the street, and said, "Yeah, and you a married man . . . you better get away from me."

After finishing that conversation, I left. She would often call me on Friday between three and four o'clock. Usually, her information was of little value. I knew she enjoyed talking to me and it didn't take a genius to realize she had a crush on me. She would plead with me to meet her at various locations.

"Can't you bring me some Virginia Slims? I done quit those Kools after you told me about your folks getting that emphysema."

"Don't you know that all cigarettes are bad for you?"

"Yeah, like the street is good for me. Bring me some smokes, please Sgt. Loshaw. How come all you white folks have such hard names to pronounce?"

"Georgia, Loshaw only has two syllables. It's not like its Wojieckowski or something. It's Lo . . . shaw."

"Bring the cigarettes and I let you in on some good s---. Oh, I'm sorry, you don't like it when I swear, do you?

"GA, I don't like a lot of things you do. What good stuff do you have?"

She slipped into her street dialect and said, "Well, maybe I seen that William Brown y' all was lookin' for."

"GA, it's not me that wants him. It's the State of Florida that wants him."

"Sgt. Jack, come on by and see me."

"Okay, hang tight and I'll come by."

I walked the block over to Greektown and bought a couple of packs of Virginia Slims for GA. By that time, my partner Cal Noles had gone home. So, I drove over to the lovely section of town we cops called Hooker Haven. It was a six-block area with the main street being Woodward Avenue, running from Clairmont to Pingree. In that small area there were more prostitutes, pimps, gamblers, he-shes, dopers, and general riff-raff than you could shake a stick at. I could only imagine how difficult it would have been for the census takers to get an accurate count. Ninety-nine percent of the street people were black, but half the clientele were white, with a large percentage Canadian. It made it easy being there with my Ontario plates.

I found Georgia at the corner of Woodward and Pingree. She came over to the opened passenger window and pretended that I was a trick.

"You sure are cute for a white devil, ain't you?"

"You trying to make me blush, Georgia?"

"Sgt. Jack, you still looking for that William Brown?"

"Sure."

"Well, he was up here earlier today, but I couldn't break away to call you, you know. I mean it was like rush hour up here with that bunch of white boys from Windsor. They sure do like the 'sisters,' know what I mean?"

"Yeah, there's no accounting for taste."

"That's mean, Sgt. Jack."

"You're right, I'm sorry."

"See, that's why I like you. You mean it when you say you're sorry. Ain't no cop ever said 'I'm sorry' to me."

"Yeah, I'm one of a kind. Okay, Georgia, tell me about William Brown."

"He looks just like his picture, but says his name is Robert or somethin'."

"Was he alone?"

"Yeah, he was in some old raggity lookin' blue car. It was all beat up and stuff."

"Make sure you call me next time you see him."

"Okay. Why don't you call me, or come by and see me when you're not working or something."

"Georgia, I'm a married man with furniture."

"What's furniture got to do with anything?"

"Never mind, just stay in touch."

I asked her if she needed any change for the phone call and she said, "Heck, I've made nearly three hundred dollars today. I don't need no chump change."

I gave her the cigarettes and told her to call me the minute she laid eyes on William Brown again.

And then she asked me a puzzling question. "You ever get scared Sgt. Jack?"

"Not me, lady. I'm bulletproof."

"Nah, you jest like any other man in some ways. I know you gotta get scared once in a while."

"GA, I'm fine, you don't need to worry about me."

"You gonna think I'm crazy, but I got to tell you that once in a while I even pray for you. I don't want nothin' happenin' to you. Who knows, some day I might need a favor."

For a moment, I wanted to jump out of my car and hug her. What a mixture, a street girl offering prayers for me, and me, a cop, wanting to hug her for saying one of the sweetest things I had ever heard.

I told her I had to go and as I put the car in drive I said to her, "Thank you, Georgia, you be careful too."

***

As usual, Georgia called the next Friday with her request for cigarettes. However, on Tuesday, May 11th, she called and there was excitement in her voice.

"William Brown was just here. He came on up to me and I know that's the guy you was lookin' for. He's stayin' above a bar at the corner of St. Anne and Woodward."

"Is it above Shooter's Bar?"

"Yeah, that's the one."

"Thanks GA. If this works out I get you a carton of Slims.

"That's all I get? A carton? I figured this was some sort of bad dude that you wanted and was hoping for more than a carton."

"GA, I appreciate you looking out for me, but if I give you more than a carton for this Florida guy, what am I gonna give you for a real legitimate Detroit bad guy?"

"How about a date with a Detroit detective?"

"Let me talk to my wife about that."

"You just have to ruin stuff, don't you?"

"We'll talk later."

***

Earlier that day I had picked up a fresh case and couldn't make it to the St. Anne's address. Actually, the place was just outside of Detroit in the city of Highland Park, so I called the Highland Park Police Department and talked to an old cop friend named Harmon Killian. He said that he would have a couple of his men check on Mr. Brown.

The next day, at 10:30 a.m., Harmon and a fellow officer walked into my office with a handcuffed William Brown. Harmon made out the arrest report and turned him over to me. After advising Mr. Brown of his constitutional rights, I began the interview.

"Do you have any idea why you are here?"

"None. The sign said this is homicide right? I sure ain't killed nobody."

"Tell me about yourself. What schools, what troubles, what friends—all that stuff."

"I went to 10th grade at Northern. My auntie raised me. I got two kids. I ain't been in no real trouble. I scuffle around and pick up work here and there. What's this about?"

"You ever hear of a man named Sherman Thompson?"

"No. Should I know him?"

"You ever hear of a man named Patrick Witton?"

"No, don't know him either."

"You ever been to Tennessee?"

"Tennessee, man I never even been out of Michigan, 'cept to go to Canada once in a while."

"Do you have any people down south?"

"None I know of."

"So, if you've never been out of Michigan then it's safe to say you've never been to Florida. Right?"

"No, I've never been there either."

"It's kind of strange, don't you think, that Dade County—that's the area around Miami, has a double murder warrant out for you?"

"You got things wrong man. It can't be me. I ain't never killed no one. I aint's ever even been to no Dade County. You got to help me, man."

He looked scared and started shaking and crying.

"Man, this is some deep s---. I didn't kill no one. What is going on? Why you doin' this to me, man? You know there's a bunch of William Browns in this world."

"William, this isn't made up. They got you by fingerprints."

"Well, they is wrong. Those can't be my prints. I ain't never been to Florida."

"William, I'm not doing anything to you. Let's talk."

I went over to the coffee pot and poured two cups. His hands were shaking so badly that coffee was spilling over onto the desk.

"Take it easy, William."

"Yeah, right, take it easy. This is like a bad dream. This can't be happening to me. What can I do, man?"

"Just settle down. I'm going to have to go out and talk to your people, you know."

William Brown was very convincing. For me to handle this thing right I was going to try to locate someone who could verify that he didn't have friends or relatives in Florida.

I spent the next hour and a half talking to Brown about his friends, his jobs, his lady friends, his habits, his kids, his hangouts, and his family. I called some of his references. No one could place him or any of his relations in the state of Florida. He was believable and it was looking like Dade County had erred. It was now past 2 p.m. and I was starving.

"William, you hungry?"

"Yeah, I haven't ate since last night."

"Okay, let's go for a ride."

I removed Brown's handcuffs and gave him my best 'Dirty Harry' look, trying to convince him that I could be cold-blooded.

"William, I hope I won't have to shoot you, so don't make me. You understand?"

"Yes sir. Ain't no way that's gonna happen. I'll be cool."

We went down to the garage and jumped into the unmarked car I was assigned. I drove over Gratiot Avenue, stopping at a Burger King. I knew I was taking a huge risk by leaving headquarters with the man likely responsible for a double murder in Florida but I had complete control of him. I also believed if he really had killed those men, this course of action, buying him a hamburger, would be the best chance to gain a confession. I was well aware that witnesses could lose their enthusiasm for telling the truth as time passed. And I knew they couldn't be trusted. Then a terrible thought crossed my mind. If my boss found out about this caper, I would be out walking a beat until my retirement date arrived. This would happen unless my loving boss killed me first. My confidence had turned to arrogance, but I believed I was doing the right thing.

William and I walked in to Burger King and up to the counter. I had two fingers on his belt at his back and felt in command. We ordered and I asked William if he was paying the bill. He gave a silly smile and said, "Heck, man, I ain't got but twenty cents on me."

"Don't worry William, I'll pay the bill. . . but you owe me." We sat down to eat and talk. I took a chance and told a lie.

"William, why did you lie to me?"

"I didn't lie to you, I swear, I didn't."

"You told me that you didn't have people in Florida, didn't you."

"Yeah, I don't."

"That's not what I've been hearing."

"Who told you that?"

"It doesn't matter. What matters is that you lied to me."

His face brightened some and a little smirk came on his face. He said, "You been knowin' all the time that I was lying, huh?"

In reality, he had me wondering whether or not he had ever been to Florida. Things pointed to it, but I didn't have a lot of faith in LEIN messages or Dade County. Here I sat with the partial remains of a burger in my hand, mustard at the corner of my mouth, practically taken in by this little gangster. I saw myself as a tough homicide detective, choking on lunch as this street punk confessed to me.

All the while I was thinking, "This job is no place for the gullible. I must be losing it." Then in an attempt to sound in charge I said, "William, I'm paid to listen to people that lie and cover-up. Did you really think that you could lie your way out of this?"

"Nah, I guess not. But I really had you going when I was crying and stuff didn't I?"

"You were pretty good."

"Well, here's how it jumped off."

He took a big bite of his burger and washed it down with a gulp of pop.

"I was in this bar, down in Miami, and these two sissy looking dudes decided that I must have looked like some sort of chump or something. These guys thought they was bad, you know? They must have thought I was some kind of country hick from the backwoods. They came up and said that they wanted my stuff."

"What stuff?"

"I had a little weed on me, just personal stuff, you know. These guys were acting like Humphrey Bogart or something , and started pushing me around and stuff, and like the big guy, Sherman, came out with a gun, started saying how he was gonna do me and stuff. Next thing that jumped off was I got all up in his face and got a holt of his gun and both of them got themselves shot."

"Did you have a gun of your own?"

"No, I'm telling you the truth this time. They got shot with their own d--- gun."

"How many shots did you fire?"

"I dunno. Maybe a few."

"Where's the gun?"

"Man, I threw that thing in a dumpster and headed back to Detroit."

"When did you get back to Detroit?"

"It took about a week. My car kept breakin' down, but it got me here.

"How well did you know the men that you shot?"

"I hardly knew then at all. I shot a little pool with them and smoked a little weed with them, that's all. They shouldn't been messin' with me. All I did was defend myself, right?"

"Sounds like self-defense to me, William."
"I was pretty sure you weren't believin' me back at your office, were you?"

"Like I said, you did a good acting job, but no, I didn't believe you."

"You think I'm going to prison. Man, they got the death penalty in the south don't they?"

"Not for cases of self-defense."

I was anxious to get Mr. Brown back to Homicide before he realized how desperate the situation really was. We finished our lunch and drove back to headquarters and William was in a great mood. My biggest worry was that my boss, Ross Barnett, would see me walking around with a murderer that I had just taken to lunch.

***

When we got back, I sat Brown across from me and typed out his self-serving confession. It went on for about an hour and filled three full pages. He made it clear that he had done only what he had to do. The two men were dead because they had messed with one bad Detroiter.

I had him booked and taken to the 9th floor cellblock where he waited two days until the crew from Florida arrived. I gave them my paperwork and had Brown brought down to Homicide. In the two days of his incarceration his heart had hardened, after some wise counsel from fellow prisoners, and he refused to talk to the two detectives, Munoz and Callebro. The detectives assured me that I wouldn't be needed to testify, since there were several eyewitnesses to the killings.

Several months went by and I had forgotten the Brown case. On September 7, 1978, I received a phone call from an Assistant District Attorney from Florida.

"Sergeant Loshaw, this is Prosecutor Benjamin Phillip down here in Florida, how ya' doin'?"

"I'm alright. What's up?"

"Sergeant, we need you to come down here and testify in the William Brown case."

"What do you need me for? I was told you had a bunch of eyewitnesses."

"Yeah, well you know how that goes. Seems that most of them have gotten cases of amnesia. We got lots of witnesses, but none of them saw anything. We can still put a case together, but it's pretty weak. We need you down here to get his confession into evidence."

"Didn't he talk to your detectives?"

"No, he wouldn't give them the time of day."

"Well, I'm not looking forward to going to Miami in September. Can't you get this thing adjourned until January?"

"I wish I could for your sake. I'll tell you what, if you will come down here we'll pay for your girlfriend or significant other to join you."

"I don't have a girlfriend or a significant other, but I bet my wife would like to come along."

"That'll be fine, sergeant. We're also going to need the arresting officer,

Harmon Killian, and his partner to come down, too. We'll make all the arrangements and expect to have you here on Monday the eleventh. Okay?"

"You got yourself a deal, Mr. Phillip."

On the tenth, the four of us flew down to Miami where Dade County's finest greeted us and drove us to our hotel. The next morning we were escorted to the courthouse. After sitting around for just over an hour we were told that the case had been adjourned for a day. The next day we learned the case was adjourned, again, for a day. My wife was quickly learning how exciting it was to go court and sit around waiting for the slow wheels of justice to turn. This place was starting to remind me of the Frank Murphy Hall of Justice in Detroit. There are many reasons court cases never seem to go as scheduled and I was always told, "Every delay is in favor of the defense."

Wednesday finally rolled around and I was informed that I would be deposed concerning the confession that Mr. Brown had given to me. Our kids had already been without their mother for three full days, so Pat flew back to Detroit. I went to the Prosecutor's Office.

I was sworn in and went about answering the questions of the prosecutor and Mr. Brown's attorney. I wouldn't describe Brown's attorney as impressive or high-powered. He was very much a gentleman, with a disarming southern twang to his voice, a pleasant smile (that concerned me), and overall, a nice demeanor. His name was Hadley Yarrow. He must have asked me fifty questions concerning the statement. He kept shaking his head, and ran his fingers through his hair constantly. Finally, he mumbled, "Sergeant, I have to tell you that I believe every word you've said. Now, please, this is off the record—my client has told you things that he won't even tell me. I know as well as you do that he is probably guilty. Actually, I have no doubt. You would think that he'd be smart enough to at least tell me the truth, wouldn't you?"

I almost felt sorry for the poor man, but wondered where he was going. I looked at the prosecutor who had raised his eyebrows.

The advocate continued, "Sergeant, after having met you and talked to you, I have to believe that you didn't scare the truth out of him. You don't come across as one of those kinds of guys. But I am almost convinced that you must have done something to get him to trust you the way he did. Would you mind telling me, what you did that made him confide in you?"

I looked at the prosecutor, who said, "Mr. Yarrow, this is off the record, correct?"

"Yes, it's just for me."

With that the prosecutor nodded and I think he wanted the answer too.

"It really wasn't anything special that I did, Mr. Yarrow. The only answer I can give you was that I reached in my pocket and bought the man a hamburger. I guess there's something to be said about catching more flies with sugar than with vinegar." I didn't bring up the fact that I took him without handcuffs to a fast-food place for his lunch.

"Well, I can't argue with your results. I think you're right, sergeant, I think you're right."

The next day, Thursday afternoon, I was notified that a plea agreement had been worked out. Mr. Brown pled to two counts of manslaughter and at sentencing he was given eight to fifteen years. Brown had escaped the death penalty and in all probability would be free before he reached the age of forty.

Chapter Six: He Killed the Helpless

Esther Lemenski was a very thin seventy-six-year-old woman who lived alone in an upper flat on Emerson Street. She and her husband had lived on the east side for over thirty years until he passed away four years ago, leaving her alone and lonely.

She had witnessed many changes in her neighborhood, but with her ready smile and pleasant attitude, her neighbors were nice to her in many ways. Her sidewalk was always cleared of snow and the neighbor boys kept her grass cut. Usually, someone would escort her to the grocery store and even help with her purchases. She was just the kind of person that people seemed eager to help, plus she was a good tipper.

February 26, 1978, was not a typical day. It was just before 11 a.m. when Esther was left to fend for herself as she walked the three blocks to the grocery store. After filling three large bags, the manager agreed to allow her to take the grocery cart home with her. She stopped at the front of her home and a young man approached and offered to carry her bags up to her flat. She was fortunate again to have someone looking out for her.

Three days later her son, Stanley, who had been unable to reach her by phone, drove over to her place. The empty shopping cart was still blocking the front porch and Stanley found the door unlocked. As he entered the upstairs doorway, he called out to her. He opened the entry door and saw the three grocery bags sitting on the kitchen table. As he walked around the table he came across his mother's lifeless body. She was lying on the kitchen's linoleum floor, her face barely recognizable and there was the beginning of a sickeningly pungent odor, of the decomposing body.

She was still wearing her long winter coat and had a traditional babushka around her head. Her winter boots were still on and water stains were near them. Her nose was bent at a severe angle and large amounts of blood had poured from it saturating her coat. She had been dead for three days. Stanley fell to the floor and cursed himself for not being a better son.

Weeks after the incident I looked at the scene photos and wondered how her son could have dealt with the horror of seeing his mother lying there, in a still and empty house, with caked blood covering her face. My stomach tightened as I thought of him and his mother, trying to imagine the evil that had happened. There were no signs of robbery and, thankfully, the poor woman had not been sexually assaulted. The question that begged to be answered was, "Who would do this?"

The case was assigned to Sergeants Charley Bix and Bob Skurda. Officially, it was Homicide File 65-83. The cause of death was determined to be from multiple head and facial traumas. The detectives worked the case diligently for several weeks, but with little evidence and no suspects, it remained unsolved. The case was then "put on the shelf" with other unsolved cases, and the detectives were assigned to new ones.

April 23, 1978

Easter Sunday

It was a perfect Michigan day with temperatures in the low seventies. There were a few fluffy clouds in the sky and the sun was bright. Emilio Brigliani, ninety years old, and his eighty-six year old wife, Sophia, were driven to the Easter service by their sixty-five year old son, Giorgio. After the service, Giorgio dropped his parents off at their home on Ashland Street. It was just after 10:30 a.m. and such a nice day that the Brigliani's decided to allow some fresh spring air into their home by leaving the front door open with only the screen door protecting the entrance.

Mr. Brigliani had busied himself preparing a pasta dish for himself and his wife. Sophia had the ironing board out and was in the process of taking wrinkles out of some clothes when it began.

An hour later, their daughter, Rosa Maglie, phoned her parents to wish them a happy Easter. The phone rang many times and Rosa re-dialed thinking she might have misdialed. It rang again without an answer. She called Giorgio and he told her he would drive over to make sure that everything was okay.

He drove to the house and realized immediately that something was wrong. He saw the ironing board lying on its side in the living room as he peered through the front door screen. He walked into the dining room to discover the most gruesome sight a son could imagine. His mother's lifeless body was laying face up on the floor with dried blood covering her battered face. His father's body was face down about six feet away on the kitchen floor. Large pools of blood covered his face, surrounding his head and saturating his clothing. He, too, had been beaten to death. Giorgio turned his father's face only to find that that his eyes were swollen shut.

Sophia's Sunbeam iron had been the weapon that formed triangular marks upon her husband's skull. The killer had used the iron and cord like a cowboy would use a lasso. Autopsies would later confirm that both had died from blunt force injuries. Mr. Brigliani had also sustained several broken ribs and a dislocated right shoulder. There were also scrape marks on his right hand, indicating that he had attempted to defend himself.

Two blocks away from the Brigliani's address, Edna Baker, age sixty-eight, was visiting her older sister, Hazel Croft. Edna had flown in from San Jose, California, two days earlier to spend Easter with her sister. On returning home from church, they heard a noise coming from the half-bath that was just inside the side-door entrance. Someone had entered the house and was washing his hands in the sink. Soon neighbors heard screams coming from the house and called the police. Upon arrival, Hazel Croft was found beaten to death in the rear bedroom and Edna Baker was found at the foot of the basement stairs. Baker was still alive and was blood was running from her nose. A jagged cut above her right eye was pouring blood. She was gently carried by the responding officers to their scout car and rushed to St. John Hospital, where she was listed as being on the "downside of critical."

Are You Busy?

My wife, Pat, and I and our four kids had just arrived home from going to the

Easter service at church. We were expecting family over for dinner at 2 p.m. when the phone rang.

"Jack, this is Inspector Barnett, are you busy?"

"Well, we have a gang coming over for dinner in a few minutes."

"Yeah, well, we just had two old people killed over on Ashland Street and another victim killed just a block away on Marlborough. There was a second victim at the Marlborough address who is still alive and over at St. John's in critical condition. I need you to meet Tim Dowell over at the hospital to get some information from her. She's an older lady and in very critical condition. Do what you can to talk to her before she dies. Is everything clear?"

"Yeah, boss. I'll get over right away."

"Sorry to interrupt your dinner Jack, but this is a bad one and we need all the help we can get."

I told Pat what was going on and that I had to go. She had that wifely look that said, "You've gotta be kidding," and then asked, "How long do you think you will be gone?"

"Well, I wouldn't hold dinner for me. I'll get back as soon as I can."

I knew it would be a while before I would see her and the kids again. I hoped she understood and then thought, "For a smart girl, she sure made a mistake marrying a cop."

***

Tim Dowell was a tough Irish detective who took his work very seriously. He was waiting for me at the hospital security entrance when I arrived. I knew most of the security people because most had retired from the department. Tim reached out his hand to me and, in his eagerness, started talking a hundred miles an hour.

"Can you believe it? Easter Sunday and they call us up for this. Man, we'll be lucky to get home by the fourth of July."

"I wouldn't worry too much, Tim. I'm sure we'll have this done before Memorial Day."

He smiled and said, "Jack, I would like you to talk to the lady, okay? I hate the smell of hospitals."

"No problem, Tim. You probably don't even like the smell of the autopsy room either."

"Are you kidding, I hate it there, too."

We walked into the critical care unit and were met by a stern looking nurse.

"You gentlemen have clearance to be in here?"

"We're from Homicide. We want to interview Edna Baker."

"No way. She's in her bed resting and can't even talk. You'll have to wait."

"Can you give us her condition?"

"She's extremely critical and unlikely to make it."

"Can we talk to her doctor?"

It was clear that she didn't want us going over her head and said, "I'm not sure that he's still here. Why don't you just go out to the waiting room and..."

"Look ma'am, whoever attacked this lady has already murdered three other people today. We have to *try* to talk to her. We need her to tell us whatever she can. The killer is out there and as far as we know, Mrs. Baker is the only one who can describe him."

49

She quickly apologized and took us to an area enclosed by white curtains where Mrs. Baker was lying. She had undergone emergency room treatment and her head was wrapped in white gauze and tape. She was attached to a ventilator and an aluminum tube was taped to her mouth. Both of her eyes were blackened but were slightly open. Her nose had an area where two inches of flesh had been gouged out.

I knew that an interview would likely be hopeless but decided to try.

"Mrs. Baker, we're from the police department. I'm going to ask you a couple of questions. I'm going to hold your hand. I will ask *yes* and *no* questions only. If the answer is yes, then please squeeze my hand. If it's no, then don't do anything."

I had to find out if she was even able to hear me, so I asked her the most obvious "yes" question I could think of.

"Is your name Edna Baker?"

To my surprise, she squeezed my hand very lightly.

"Do you know my name?"

She squeezed lightly again. This wasn't working. I had to ask one more question. It looked like this poor lady was struggling to keep her eyes open.

"Are you hungry?"

She squeezed again.

"Well, Tim, I don't think she can help us right now."

The Marlborough Scene

We walked out quietly and drove over to the Marlborough scene.

The house was a one and half story bungalow. It was right off the alley behind Mack Avenue and it appeared that the murderer had entered through the side screen door, which had apparently been left unlocked. Once you stepped inside the side door there was a half-bath where small amounts of blood were splattered on the sink, the soap dish, and on a hand towel. It seemed that whoever had committed this crime had walked into the house to wash the blood away, came across the victims, and did what he did.

We had the evidence technicians take blood samples from all stains for comparison purposes. Helen Kroft's body was still in the first floor front bedroom. She was a slightly built woman with very thin arms. Three of the fingers on her right hand were broken and bent at ninety-degree angles. She was lying face down, fully clothed, alongside a fully made bed. Her face was so battered that the thought crossed my mind that the perpetrator had grabbed her by her hair and slammed her face repeatedly onto the floor. The scene was grotesque with blood, skin, and mucus spread on the floor. I was thankful that there was nothing to indicate any sexual violation. I told everyone to leave the room. I sat on a chair in the bedroom and tried to imagine all that had happened. I examined every area of the room as I thought of frail Mrs. Kroft as she faced her killer. I wondered what her thoughts were, and I wondered what hatred the killer must have had to bring such violence and damage to an older, innocent, and helpless person. Throughout the years, I had witnessed many brutal homicides, but this one exceeded any of the rest. My hope was that our victim was unconscious during the worst part of the assault.

I tried to think of any reasonable motive and struck out. Was this killing just for the sake of killing? There were no signs of a robbery, no signs of sexual assault, no signs of retribution, no signs of betrayal . . . there were no signs of anything that I could see. What kind of person would do this?

I finally walked out of the bedroom. I told Tim Dowell that this was plain savagery that went beyond anything I had seen. The tough Irishman said to me, "Jack, I've gotta get out of here. I'm gonna go sell real estate or used cars or something."

"Tim, it can't get much worse than this. Why don't we go outside and see if there's anything out there?"

"Jack, this one doesn't make sense at all."

"I don't think reason has anything to do with this. I'll finish the inside stuff and then we'll head over to the scene on Ashland to check on the other murders. You gonna be okay?"

"Yeah, I'm good."

The Ashland Scene

When Tim and I arrived at the scene of the Brigliani murders on Ashland, most of the scene investigation had been completed. We talked to the remaining officers, looked things over, talked to a few neighbors, and drove to 1300 Beaubien-police headquarters.

A very unusual item was found at the home on Ashland. A man's silver ring with a large turquoise type stone was sitting on the floor near Mrs. Brigliani's body. It looked cheap and gaudy. I had it measured and it was a size twelve and spun freely on my ring finger. If it had been dropped by the killer, it would appear that he was a large man. During the course of the investigation, the ring was shown to every member of the family and all agreed that it did not belong to Mr. Brigliani.

I took the ring to a couple of jewelry stores and pawnshops. It was valued at less than a hundred dollars. I had a photo taken of the ring and it was published in the *Detroit News* and the *Detroit Free Press*. After that, I showed the ring to various members of the specialized bureaus in the department. Sergeant Dick Myers from the Gang Squad mentioned that it looked similar to those worn by members of some motorcycle gangs. Interestingly enough, across the street from the Brigliani's home, living in an upper flat, was a rather obnoxious lad by the name of Walter Krevchuck. He was one of the rising stars of the Vigilante Motorcycle Club. The club's headquarters was only three miles south of our scene.

Mr. Krevchuck went by the street name "Confusion" and I was looking forward to interviewing this genius.

The scene photographs from both addresses were developed and brought to me. I spent an hour going through them and another hour re-reading the witness and police statements. My stomach and eyes were burning, and I thought, "maybe eight cups of coffee *was* too much." Finally, it was time for lunch. I was surprised to see that it was already 11:30 PM and one of the only places opened on a Sunday night was a Coney Island restaurant on Lafayette Street in downtown Detroit. I figured that a little more acid would probably hasten my death, but having already lived to the age of thirty-five, how many more years could a man expect?

"Tim, have you thought about eating?"

"Only for the last four hours."

"Coney Island okay?"

"Well, you gotta die of something, sure."

So we feasted on two Coneys, light onions, and went back to Homicide. I pulled some of the Vigilante names from the Gang Squad and ran them through the Identification Section. They were a collection of rogues! Walter "Confusion" Krevchuck had two and a half pages of prior cases on his record. He was strictly a small timer with arrests for marijuana possession, petty theft, possession of stolen property, and fourteen driving infractions. He didn't appear to have the background that would catapult him to murder. Physically he was 6'3" and weighed in at a rotund 290 pounds. I thought the ring might fit nicely on his hand.

As 3 a.m. was approaching, Tim and I headed over to Walter's flat. The house was dark. As Tim knocked several times with his flashlight, lights came on. We heard footsteps coming down the stairs. The door opened and there stood Walter, with bare feet, baggy boxers, scraggly beard, hair going in nine different directions, blood-shot eyes, and a heavy odor of alcohol on his breath. His belly extended several inches over his belt line and I knew he had

lied about his true weight . . . he easily tipped the scale at 350 pounds.
We showed him our badges and he cordially invited us in. I looked into the living room and realized that Walter was in no danger of winning the *Good Housekeeping* award for cleanliness. I had seen burglarized homes in neater condition than ol' Walter's.

He didn't seem surprised to see us. He lived up to his name, however, and acted confused. I think life in general confused poor Walter. We sat down and tried to talk to him, but he was scurrying around trying to hide the remains of some not-quite-finished joints in the ashtrays. I took out the ring and asked Confusion to try it on.

"Man, what's this about?"

I glared at him and said, "Just try on the ring."

"If it fits, do I get to keep it, man? Hee, hee, hee."

I thought to myself, this guy must think he's Cinderella.

"Just try it on, Walter."

"Sure, man, it's a good lookin' ring."

Obviously, his taste in jewelry was impeccable, and I said, "Yeah, I was thinking of getting a matching pair for my wife and me."

"You married, man?"

"Just try on the ring, Walter."

Finally, after admiring the ring for several more seconds he tried it on. Even though he was obese his fingers were skinny and the ring spun like a hula hoop on each of his digits. Then he suggested that it might fit on another of his appendages. I let him know that we weren't interested in seeing the fit.

We questioned him about his activities in the last few days and said goodbye to Walter. I told him not to leave town without notifying the sanitation department and apologized for waking him.

"That's alright, man. I had to get up in a few hours anyhow. What time is it, man?"

"Don't worry, Walter, time is just a way of keeping track of days."

Walter looked like he understood what I had just said. That really made me nervous.

"Walter?"

"Call me Confusion, man."

"Have you seen a ring like this before, Walter?"

"Maybe down at the Club or somethin'. I really don't know, man. Ya' know lots of guys wear rings ya' know, and lots of broads wear 'em too. And you should see the tattoos man, we got this gal . . ."

With that, we headed out the door.

We drove back to Homicide, filed a few things away, drank another cup of coffee, and decided that it was time to close up the shop. It was after 6:30 a.m. and the sun was trying to rise through the morning haze. It scorched my eyes as I drove home. I needed a couple hours of sleep before heading back. The kids were busying themselves with breakfast before school, while Pat was getting ready to take her turn as the carpool driver. One peck on the cheek from her and I crashed.

I tossed and turned, hammered the poor pillow for four hours, and finally crawled out of bed. My stomach was still on fire and my head was pounding. I swallowed two aspirins and, being a glutton for punishment, sucked down two cups of coffee. Pat made a nice brunch and I promised to get home early as I walked out the door and headed back to 1300 Beaubien.

Once I arrived downtown, I phoned St. John Hospital and was told that Mrs. Baker was holding her own, but was still in critical condition. I couldn't interview her for a couple of days. The fact that she was still alive was certainly a good sign. I checked a few phone tips that had come in and several people reported that it was either a Mafia payback or a drug deal gone wrong. So much for tips. The only thing I had working was a few fingerprints. We had several partial prints left at both scenes so I had all the family members brought in for elimination fingerprints. I had the prints taken to the Identification Section and I knew that it would be a time consuming, and usually futile, process.

The next significant event happened on Wednesday afternoon. Tim and I drove over to the hospital on the chance of re-interviewing Mrs. Baker. We were pleased that she was conscious, her eyes were open, and she seemed somewhat alert. I introduced myself again and spoke to her regarding the incident. She hadn't been told that her sister had died and I feared that she would ask about it. She tried to speak, but nothing came out. So, again, I went to the squeezing hand method. I told her I would ask only yes and no questions. "Yes" would need one squeeze and "no" would need no squeezes. I asked if she understood and she gave me one squeeze.

"Was there more than one person who did this to you and your sister?"

One squeeze.

"Were there two people?"

One squeeze.

After two yes answers in a row, I needed her to respond negatively.

"Were there more than two people?"

She never twitched.

"Is your answer 'no?'"

She squeezed my hand gently.

"Were the two men black?"

No response.

"Were the two men white?"

She gave a firm squeeze to my hand. It seemed incredible to me that there was more than one person who could have done such a thing. I could imagine one person, being out of his mind, but for two men to do what had been done was beyond belief. I was dumbfounded.

"Let's talk about one of the men. Would you say that he was a young man?"

No response.

"Was he between thirty and forty years of age?"

A gentle squeeze.

"Let's try to describe how he was dressed. Was he in casual clothes?

No response.

"Was he dressed like a business person, suit, tie, that kind of thing?"

She gave a squeeze.

This was not making sense. What did we have? A couple of well-dressed men out there killing people. Had they just left the Easter service? And then she fell asleep.

I looked at Tim and he was shaking his head. We walked out of the room.

"Jack, does that make any sense?"

"None of this is making any sense. Have you ever heard of two men in suits killing people? I'm afraid that Mrs. Baker has had her brain really scrambled."

We drove back downtown and felt as confused as "Confusion" had ever been. I stopped at Latent Prints and told them to concentrate on the prints of white men. I hoped that the ring belonged to the killer and it might have been similar to the ones worn by the motorcycle dudes. There were lots of questions going through my head. How many motorcycle guys go around in suits? My head was hurting and I was finding it hard to believe that Mrs. Baker was right.

***

Sometimes there is a fine line between right and wrong. It may be very fine, but it is never invisible.

We needed to get into the Vigilante Motorcycle Club. Generally speaking, the police and motorcycle gang members were not on speaking terms. A knock on the door would have been met with laughter. I didn't have enough probable cause to get a search warrant and so it remained a closed door. "What to do? What to do?"

The gang met every Saturday night at the clubhouse at Gratiot and McClellan. On a normal Saturday night, there would be over a hundred members in attendance. The usual activities included smoking pot, dropping acid, guzzling beer, playing cards, listening to heavy rock, trading guns and sometimes women, and of course, talking about their *hogs.* This particular Saturday night was special. A tattoo artist was on the premises to decorate a couple of the women in very delicate areas of the anatomy. All the fellas were eagerly awaiting the grand event.

Tim and I discussed the various ways of getting into the joint. After racking our brains, and struggling with our consciences, we decided on a *slightly* improper way of gaining entry. I invited Sergeant Henry Cox and his crew of three very large and energetic police officers to join us in the "raid." It was 9:30 p.m. and we were a few blocks away from the clubhouse. We could see that there were fifty to sixty bikes parked in front of the establishment. There was a pay phone on the corner and someone "dropped a dime." I'm sure that our Founding Fathers would have rolled over in their graves at such a thing . . . so much for those constitutional rights.

"Police emergency."

"I don't mean to be no snitch, man, but there's been a shootin' at the Vigilantes, man."

"What's the location, sir?"

"Gratiot and McClellan."

The caller hung up the phone and within seconds the police dispatcher gave out a run.

"Scout 15-5 and Scout 15-3, Gratiot and McClellan, the Vigilante Motorcycle Club, a shooting. 15-70 (the sergeant's code) you make the scene also."

The notified crews responded and then Tim spoke over our radio.

"Homicide 2794 to dispatch, we are just down the street, mark us out of service to Gratiot and McClellan."

Cox chimed in. "MCMU #1 is on the way also."

We, along with Cox and his crew, were there in a few moments and soon the precinct units arrived. We asked two of the uniformed officers to knock on the front door and had Cox and one of his men go to the back door. A startled looking gang member opened the door and said, "This is a private party, you can't come in."

The uniformed officer, who was quite eager to show us some of his street toughness said, "I suppose it's by invitation only. Get out of the way before you become a doormat."

With that the "doorman" stepped aside and we went barging in. The place reeked with the sickeningly sweet smell of pot. There were over a hundred people inside and most were unaware of our presence. Henry Cox and his crew came in from the back and Cox pulled the plug from the jukebox. Moans and groans were heard and complaints of, "Who turned off the music, man?"

Some of the club patrons soon realized that uninvited and unwelcomed guests were on the scene. A couple of guns and three knives hit the floor, a few who were still sober enough walked to the johns and rear exits. Marijuana and assorted pills were falling like snowflakes to the floor. Before it was over we had made twelve arrests and conveyed some of the most obnoxious ones to Homicide to be interviewed. No one had a ring that looked anything like the one left at the murder scene. All that we really accomplished that night was harassing a bunch of losers, who were immune to insults, but all the same, it wasn't too bad a way to spend a Saturday night. I was delighted that some of the club women actually had more than ten teeth. "Confusion" was there and, to my surprise, was certainly one of the brightest ones in the bunch. He let me know that we were always welcome at his place and could even bring our women with us.

***

It was clear to me that most of the police brass were pleased that the suspects were Caucasians . . . a racial situation would only have inflamed the scared community. The officers at Latent Prints were having no success in matching the prints from the scene. A couple of weeks went by and they had eliminated white guys by the hundreds with still no matchups. For a brief time it seemed like it was an open season for uniformed cops to bring in every white punk strolling the east side. Every morning there was some white guy waiting for me to interrogate him. My boss, Ross Barnett, received a call from the captain of the Grosse Pointe Police Department, who said, "Inspector Barnett, I wanted to tell you that whatever your men are doing, please keep it up. We haven't even had a garbage can tipped over since your men started leaning on these white guys. If this keeps up I'm going to have to lay off a few of my men."

***

"I'd rather be lucky than good." —*Yogi Berra*

Most homicide cases are solved within the first forty-eight hours. I had worked this one for twenty-four straight days. I was physically tired, my brain was worn out, and even my soul needed a day off. It was grueling and there were nights when I woke up in the middle of my sleep thinking about older people being beaten to death. What scared me more than anything was the thought that the killer might take a fifth life while I was still searching for him.

Sometime during that twenty-four day period I began wondering if the slaying of Esther Lemenski was the beginning of a series of murders. She could have been the first, or perhaps there were others before her of which I was unaware. I went to work that day and checked every open homicide involving older people for the last two years, but no others fit the pattern. It seemed to me that Esther Lemenski was the first one, the Brigliani's second and third, and Helen Kroft the fourth. I had to get the killer before there was a fifth.

I talked with my boss, Ross Barnett, and told him that my gut instinct was telling me we were going in the wrong direction. The viciousness, senselessness, and evilness of these brutal acts caused me to believe they might have been the result of racial hatred. Finally, on the twenty-fourth day, I went to Latent Prints and talked to the best person in that division, Traci Turrell. She was one of two female classmates in my academy class and she knew her stuff. I knew I could trust her.

"Traci, you've got to promise me that you won't tell anyone what I'm asking you to do. I know your group has been checking every white guy from age seventeen to sixty, but I want you to start checking black guys for these killings."

"You won't get in trouble for me doing this, will you Jack?"

"I will take my chances, just do it for me, okay?"

"No problem. Why so secret?"

"It's one of those political things and everyone upstairs is hoping it's not a black against white kinda thing. At this point I think we need to cover everything."

Traci was a professional and no amount of politics would get in the way of her work. I knew she would do her part. She finished by saying, "Jack, if his prints are in the system I will find them and the minute I do, you will know about it."

I gave her a smile and told her to get to work.

I took one last ride over to St. John Hospital to see Mrs. Baker. She never recovered her senses as a result of the beating and her status remained unchanged. She did manage to talk but nothing she said made any sense. From a prosecution standpoint, she had little value. As I thought about her and the description she gave of the two killers, it became clear to me that she was actually describing Tim Dowell and me. I think our images were etched into her brain when we visited her immediately after she left the emergency room. As I thought of it, I felt a sickness inside and I was amazed that no one else had been assaulted during the period when I was running around having anyone in white skin arrested. As I walked out of the hospital, I said, "We've been going the wrong way, period! Thank you Lord that no one else has been hurt so far. Please help me find this guy."

Later that day, Inspector Barnett called me into his office. We discussed the case and he ordered me to take a couple of days off. I didn't tell him about Officer Turrell checking the prints of black men and I sure didn't mention the "still small voice" that was speaking to me. I thanked him and told him I would enjoy a day or two off.

The next morning I drove the three hours to our cottage just outside of Farwell, Michigan. It was just after 11 a.m. when I pulled into the driveway. My aunt Frances, who lived two doors from our place, came running out to see me.

"Jack, your wife just called and they want you to call homicide right away."

"Thanks, can I use your phone?"

She smiled and said, "Sure, as long as you have ten cents."

I ran over to her place and called. I actually had to dial twice because my hands were shaking and I misdialed the first time. The phone rang and I was transferred to Reg Hart, my squad leader. He said, "Jack, they made the prints and you'll be surprised that they belong to a black man named Tyus Weary. The print guys must have run out of white suspects so they started checking against black men. Did you have anything to do with that?"

"Heck, I ain't that smart boss. Is he in custody?"

"No, but we got everyone out looking for him. Can you get back here tonight?"

"I have to cut the grass first, but I'll be back in less than four hours. Tell Turrell that I owe her a box of chocolates."

With that Reg said, "How did you know it was Turrell that identified the prints?"

I knew I was busted so I said, "She's the best one down there, so I assumed it was her."

I mowed the lawn and drove back to Detroit. On the way back to 1300, I thought about the thrill that Police Officer Turrell felt when the prints matched. Turrell would never get her name in the paper, and only her peers would ever appreciate what she had done. She was a cop's cop and that was all the reward she needed.

During the drive, I had another concern. What if someone were to shoot Weary before I had a chance to talk to him? I didn't want anyone even talking to him, let alone killing him, so I hurried back to work. It was also during the drive that I wondered about the life I had chosen and why God would be willing to enter my world. Was He really directing my steps? There were times when I knew He had.

I walked into homicide just before 5 p.m. Henry Cox's crew had arrested Weary and had him, safely tucked away in a guarded interrogation room, waiting for me. I was eager to meet him but before entering the room I prayed and asked God for guidance. I knew I needed the strength, patience, and whatever else it might take to deal with the person who had ended the lives of those helpless people. And, from a criminal standpoint, I needed a confession because fingerprints alone would not be enough evidence to prosecute him.

I entered the interrogation room. Weary had his right hand cuffed to the welded eye-bolt at the corner of the desk. The room was small, 10' by 12' with a 36" by 48" one-way mirror in to the wall. The room and mirror were much smaller than anything I had seen on TV or in the movies. It had been freshly painted a light green, because some defender of criminals thought it was less intimidating, and still it smelled of a sick, sweaty odor left behind by fretting suspects.

I loved the art of interrogation and I knew how important this interview would be. What if he refused to talk? What if he took the hard line attitude of "prove it was me, cop!" What if he was a total nut case and couldn't remember anything? What if I didn't ask the right questions? In the time I had searched for him, he had had time to plan his answers. I felt a lot of pressure and I prayed again that God would give me the wisdom to do things right.

Tyus Weary was only twenty-two years old, stood five foot eight, and weighed in at one hundred and eighty pounds. He had a dark complexion with no facial hair and needed a haircut to even his overgrown afro. His arms were flabby with no muscle tone to indicate any appearance that would scare anyone.

I introduced myself. He looked scared, picked at his nails, and rubbed his lips several times. He had a soft high-pitched voice and asked, "Did I do something wrong?"

"We'll talk about that in a minute. I need to bring someone else in here."

I stepped outside the door and invited a female officer, Debra McCann, from Central Photo into the room with a video camera. She was in civilian clothes and didn't look intimidating. I told Weary we were going to tape his statement. He smiled and seemed pleased about that.

I took out the Constitutional rights form and read it to him. I asked him if he understood his rights and he replied that he did. Then I asked him what I thought was an insulting question, "Can you read?"

"Yes."

"Read to me the first two points on your rights form."

He read the sentences without hesitation and I had him sign the form along with initialing each point.

"There was an older lady killed in February, do you know anything about that."

"No, I don't know nothing about that. Really I don't."

"Do you remember what you were doing on Easter Sunday?"

"I mighta went to church that day."

"What church was that?"

"I don't know the name, but it's the one up on Mack."

"Is it a Catholic church?"

"I don't even know. It's just a church, ya' know?"

"Did you go there by yourself?"

He hesitated in answering and then he said, "I don't think I went to church that day, as I think about it."

His eyes were darting around the room and I knew he was lying.

I pulled the Vigilante ring out of the evidence folder and put it on the desk.

He looked at it and tears came to his eyes.

"Tell me about the ring, Tyus."

"I'm real sorry. I didn't mean to hurt the lady."

"What lady are you talking about?"

His tears were flowing freely as he said, "The one I helped with her groceries. I saw the ring sittin' there on the table by her TV. I didn't mean to hit her so hard but I wanted that ring."

"Did you take anything else besides the ring?"

"No, sir. That's all I took, honest. It would have been real mean to take anything else."

"Why did you hit her?"

"I knew she was thinking bad things about me and I did it."

"How many times did you hit her?"

"Maybe once or twice, that's all. I couldn't believe that she fell over so fast."

I remembered reading in the autopsy protocol that Mrs. Lemenski was a slight woman who weighed ninety-seven pounds and it wouldn't have taken much of a punch to knock her over.

"Tyus, from what I saw from the photographs at the crime scene, it looked like she had been hit several times. How do you explain that?"

"She was making some noises and I didn't want the people living below her to hear it, so I had to hit her a couple more times just to keep her quiet. She didn't die, did she?"

I felt like yelling, "Yes, you moron! You beat her to death with those big fists of yours and that's why you're here at Homicide, "but I had to hide my emotions, so I asked, "How do you think we came up with the ring?"

"I s'pose you got it when I lost it."

"And, of course, it had your fingerprints on it, and where do you think we found it?"

"Probably at that other house."

"Do you want to tell me about what really happened on Easter Sunday?"

He started sobbing for several minutes and I motioned to the video operator, McCann, to keep the tape going.

"The lady with the groceries, that happened in February. Is that the first person that you ever had trouble with?"

"I swear that was the first one. I never thought I would ever hurt someone like that. I'm real sorry. Make sure you tell her for me, okay?"

"So what happened on Easter Sunday?"

"I kept expecting the police to come and get me and I stayed inside a lot, but nobody came. So I went outside and walked by that lady's house a few days later but nothing happened."

"So, there were no other people you had trouble with until Easter?"

"No, I cried a lot about that lady, but I didn't bother no one until that day.

"So, what happened?"

"I was just walking by and this lady was in her home just starin' at me. I went up to the porch to let her have a good look at me. She was ironing or something and I thought I would just talk to her."

"Did she open the door for you?"

"No, it was open and I just stepped in."

"What happened next?"

"She started yelling in some strange language for no reason. And then this man came around the corner and looked like he was going to get me so I just started swinging away. The man hit me a couple of times and then he fell over."

"Did you hit him with the iron?"

"No, I would never do nothin' like that."

"What happened next?"

"I think the woman just kinda fell over and maybe had a heart attack or somethin'. And I just walked out of there feeling real bad."

"Did you take anything from that house?"

"No, sir, nothing at all. There was no reason for her to be looking at me, that's all I know."

He started to cry again, and I told him to stop it and to continue, "What happened next?"

"I got out of there real fast and went to the alley and saw some blood on my hands and a door was open and I walked in and began washing my hands and this old lady started yelling at me."

"And then . . ."

"She wouldn't stop hollering so I told her to shut up and then I think I hit her and some other lady came at me and I think I might have hit her, too. It happened so fast and I really can't tell you any more about that. I hope they're okay. They are, aren't they?"

"Did you take anything from that house?"

"No, I would never do something like that."

At that time, I ended the interview. The video technician stood there with her eyebrows raised and a look of bewilderment on her face. And then Tyus said, "I'm so glad you're my detective, I was afraid that I would get some real mean guy."

I had to ask him one last question and I feared the answer, "Tyus, after the assaults of Easter Sunday, did you commit any other attacks?"

"No, sir. I was done after that. Are you going to let me go home?"

It had been a long time since I had smiled as I said, "No, Tyus. You're going to be with us for a long time."

"That's what I thought."

It was hard to believe that this was the man who had brought death to those elderly people. He was a young man, with his soft voice, one who seemed so gentle and yet, within his heart was buried a monster that carried evil. He seemed a bit childish, somewhat innocent and naïve. And yet he was the one responsible for murdering four seniors and leaving one with irreparable brain damage.

I dismissed the technician and sat there looking at Tyus. I wondered what it was that propelled him to commit such wickedness. He and I simply chatted for a while. He told me that his mother had left him before he entered kindergarten. He told us of being a bed-wetter until the age of twelve and how his father, Roosevelt Davis, had belittled him in front of family and friends. There was one special way that his father tormented him. He would make young Tyus stand on one foot for punishment and when he lost his balance, old Dad would smack him across his face. It didn't' matter that Tyus cried and fell down, because Dad would pick him up and force him to do it "right." Tyus would then have to ask his dad if he could switch feet and that resulted in being hit again.

Tyus cried as he repeated his father's words, "You keep wetting the bed and one of these days I'll cut it off and you won't have that problem ever again."

As Tyus told the story, his forehead wrinkled and his eyes seemed to get darker. It was clear that he hated his father. He talked about his days in school and it was obvious that he hated most people in authority. I began to believe that Tyus may have struck out against the older people as a way of getting even with the father who abused him. It was certainly a strange way to exact revenge, but I became convinced of it.

There was a huge part in me that wanted to hate the murderer of the old, helpless people, but after interrogating him, I felt some sympathy. He could never be excused for anything he did and I was pleased that he had "copped out" and would spend the rest of his life in jail, but I also ached for him.

I walked him out of the interrogation room, to the prisoner elevator, and took him to the 9th floor cellblock where I turned him over to the jail guards.

***

The following day I typed out the warrant request and took it to Assistant Prosecutor Tim Kennedy. He recommended four counts of Murder One, one count of Assault with Intent to Commit Murder, three counts of Unlawful Entry, and one count of Larceny from a Building.

Tyus Weary was brought to court for his arraignment, held without bond, and a preliminary exam was set for ten days later.

It had been a highly publicized case and when the preliminary exam date came, the media was heavily represented. The exam was straightforward and uncomplicated except for some showmanship displayed by Tyus's father. As soon as Weary was bound over for trail, Mr. Davis stood up in court and shouted, "My son didn't do none of that. It's just a frame job to put it on a black man. I'm gonna get the best lawyer that money can buy and clear him. You'll see, you'll see."

The media folks rushed out into the hallway awaiting the appearance of Roosevelt Davis. Microphones and cameras were readied, but before they could interview him, I walked up and said something very quietly to him, "The only regret I have is that you're not standing trial with your son. You and I both know that you are the main reason he killed those people. I promise you, if you say one word to these reporters, I'll expose you. Do you hear me? One word and the whole world will know . . . one word."

Then I whispered something that only he and I will ever know.

With that, Mr. Davis decided not to be interviewed. And as far as I know, he never uttered a word in public concerning the matter. One of the TV reporters asked me, "Sergeant, I don't know what you said to him and you probably did what you thought best, but would you mind telling me what you told him? We've missed out on a good interview."

"I wish I could, but now is not the time."

Would you like to know what I said?

I bet you would.

As I reviewed this case, I became so aware of how detectives often chase the "red herring." The descriptions given by the surviving victim had us looking in the wrong areas. The ring took us far from the truth and could have caused serious delays or even someone else's death. I was finally able to breathe, once again, when I realized that no one else had been hurt as a result of being misdirected. And all I could say was, "Thank you, Lord."

Chapter Seven: New Jersey, New Jersey

In the late 70s it was decided by the upper echelons that women would be allowed to transfer into the Homicide Division of the Detroit Police Department. Many of the people in power believed that solving murder cases was a job for men and men only. The thinking was that women, being the weaker sex, needed to be sheltered from the carnage that only men were fit to handle. It was a man's duty to keep women away from the wickedness of murder and being "barefoot and pregnant" was the motto. Many women were curious about when the Neanderthals would finally be eaten by dinosaurs.

Two female detectives were sent to the Homicide Unit on the same day. One was named Dorothy Reo and the other, Wendy Halsey. Wendy was a cute little blond, with cute blue eyes, cute blond hair, and a cute little figure spread over her twenty-seven-year-old body. She was the daughter of a medical doctor. Wendy explained that one of her great joys in life, while growing up in Birmingham, Michigan, was to pretend to be poor. She was educated at St. Mary's, an all-girls private school, where only the very wealthy attended. She learned to drive behind the wheel of her daddy's Porsche. One day, for no reason that her parents could ever understand, she and a couple of her girlfriends joined the Detroit Police Department soon after they had graduated from Central Michigan University. She had earned a degree in sociology and thought working with criminals would be fulfilling. Alone with her friends, Wendy had visited a minimum-security prison while in college and was convinced that life simply wasn't fair.

She knew it would be fun and exciting to go into police work. So she and her friends did just that! She was a bright young lady and graduated with honors from the police academy. She was immediately assigned to the Sex Crimes Unit where she worked for four years and thoroughly enjoyed her duties. With that experience under her belt, she decided that it would be even more exciting to work in the Homicide Unit. Her supervisors gave her a strong endorsement and soon she was one of the two females assigned to Homicide. Even though Wendy was bright and quite attractive, not all of the homicide detectives were delighted to have her aboard. During her first exposure to an autopsy at the Wayne County Morgue, she was seen racing to the restroom where violent explosive gagging noises were heard. She reappeared minutes later drained of all color.

She, along with most new detectives, was only assigned the "platter" cases, where the identity of the perpetrator was known. Platter cases were those in which very little detective work was necessary. Typically, the perpetrator was arrested at the scene and was a friend or family member. All that was required of the officer in charge was to wrap up the scene investigation, interview the witnesses, interrogate the prisoner, and prepare the warrant request. It was considered "busy" work and didn't call for a lot of investigative skills.

One of the cases that Wendy picked up was the killing of a female named Mansie Henkins. Her boyfriend, Charles Crawford, had shot her to death. Her three children, ages nine, eleven, and fourteen were eyewitnesses to the murder of their mom. Mr. Crawford fled from the scene and a NIC (not in custody) warrant was obtained for Murder in the Second Degree. Second-degree murder was one that lacked premeditation.

Several months later, Mr. Crawford was arrested in Newark, New Jersey.. His arrest caused severe anxiety among the brass of the Detroit Police Department because it was policy that the officer in charge of the case would be sent to the venue of the arrest. Now, of course, with Wendy being a female, logic reasoned that another female accompany her. However, common sense cried out that a male accompany her for safety's sake. Economic reasoning cried foul: that will mean paying for an extra room. To further complicate matters, just prior to Mr. Crawford's arrest, little Wendy had married another police officer.

My wonderful, loving, and kind boss, Inspector Ross Barnett, who was always in a hurry, charged into my office. His face was red, beads of perspiration covered his forehead, when he found me sitting at my desk. "Loshaw, there ain't a man in this unit that I trust, including you, but I have to send Wendy to New Jersey to get a prisoner and I sure as h--- can't send her with another female. You're as close to trustworthy as I have and that ain't saying much. Now, call your wife and make sure it's alright. I sure don't need some wife down here screaming for my scalp. You make sure it's okay. You hear?"

I was really enjoying watching old Ross squirm. He just wasn't much when it came to being politically correct, so I had to tease him some. "Gee, boss, my wife's pretty understanding, but this is going to really push her to the limits. Do you know any good divorce attorneys?" I knew he was experienced in that area since he was currently with wife number three.

"Well, then, you just convince her that it's standard operating procedure. I know that *I'm* not going with no woman out of state, especially one married to another cop."

I was having a field day. "Wow, do you know if her husband is the jealous type?"

"Listen Loshaw, you just make the call."

His face had reddened considerably by that time and sweat was starting to stain his white shirt.

I just couldn't let it rest. "We staying overnight, boss?"

"What do you think? Of course, and in different rooms!"

"That doesn't sound very cost-effective, sir."

"Cost-effective? You just make sure that you act right, 'cause if you don't, you won't have to worry about her husband. You'll have to worry about me."

It was difficult keeping a straight face, but I added, "It isn't me that I'm worried about boss, it's her!"

He looked like he was about to have a heart attack, so I retreated.

"You don't have to worry about me, boss. I'm a married man with furniture and I'm looking forward to visiting the great state of New Jersey."

He let out a grunt and with a crooked smile said, "Let me know what your wife has to say. By the way, Loshaw, how did you ever get such a pretty young wife? You hang around elementary schools or something?"

"It's all about animal magnetism, boss."

With that he strolled out of my office and poured himself another cup of coffee.

I telephoned my wife, Pat, and told her the whole story. She didn't sound the least bit concerned and agreed to pack my bag. I had made many trips out of state, but this would be the first with a female. I informed Barnett of my wife's approval and for the next few hours I was busy fending off the wise cracks from several of my fellow detectives. Several offered names of marriage counselors and a few handed me business cards of divorce lawyers.

The next day, Wendy and I flew out from Detroit Metropolitan Airport to New Jersey. Wendy's luggage consisted of three pieces and was the type that the gorilla banged around on the TV commercial. I carried one piece that was the type that Laurel and Hardy carted around. We arrived in Newark and were greeted by a Newark detective named Milosic, who looked sixty but was probable forty; it appeared that the streets had taken their toll on him. He gave me a wink and with that all-knowing look of a fellow conspirator said, "Nice looking partner, Mac."

I had to cool him down so I said, "Yeah, but we're not real sure about her, know what I mean?"

"Nah, you gotta be kiddin', Mac. Ain't that just the way it is? Pretty girl like her, you'd think she'd be attracted to men, you know?"

I sighed and answered, "Yeah, just my luck."

With that bit of conversation out of the way, he proceeded to talk about the problems that minorities had brought to the Newark area. Finally, we arrived at our hotel and Detective Milosic told us that he'd pick us up in the morning and take us to the jail to get our prisoner.

Wendy and I went to our rooms, freshened up, and decided to go take the bus over to midtown Manhattan. We ate at Jack Dempsey's place and afterward took the subway to the Twin Towers. The security guard didn't want to let us onto the elevator because we weren't dressed appropriately. I told him about our mission and, after showing him our badges, he not only took us to the top but he waived the two dollar admission charge.

"You two are from the Murder Capital, eh?"

"Yep, that's us. I hear that New York City is no Garden of Eden itself."

He sounded like an apologist for the city when he said, "Things really aren't that bad. We get a lot of outsiders that come into our town and raise havoc. I think we're getting a little more civilized. Plus a lot of southern people are comin' here from Puerto Rico and stuff and makin' a mess of things."

After talking to this guy for a few minutes, I understood why he was assigned to drive the elevator. At least he didn't have to ask for directions.

The sky was heavy that night and by the time we reached the top floor all we could see were misty gray clouds. We viewed the clouds for a few minutes and I was happy we had saved the cost of the entry fee. We walked around for a few minutes and enjoyed hearing the New Yorkers' accents. I looked at Wendy and said, "Well, I think this is about all the Manhattan activity I can handle. Are you ready to go back to the hotel?"

She agreed and we took the subway back to midtown and the bus to Newark. It was almost midnight when we arrived back at the hotel and I wanted to make sure that Homicide's Cinderella made it home before the witching hour. After dropping her off and checking her room for intruders, I went to my room and opened my single piece of luggage. On the top of my clothing was a note from Pat that was taped to a bag of red pistachio nuts. The note read "In case you are caught red-handed, at least you will have an excuse."

It was signed, "Love, Pat."

What a girl! I would have called her but I knew she was counting sheep by then.

The next day, Wendy and I ate breakfast in the hotel café. At 8:30 Detective Milosic arrived wearing the same wardrobe as the previous day. We piled into his city-owned car and drove over to the county jail. The prisoner, Crawford, was brought out. He was a monster of a man, standing 6'7" and weighing over 400 pounds. His wrists were gigantic and for the first time in my life, my handcuffs didn't fit my prisoner. The guard brought out a pair of plastic handcuffs that King Kong couldn't have gotten free from. I told dear Mr. Crawford, "Do you see who my partner is?"

"Yeah, I see her."

I put on my evil glare and said, "I want to tell you something, right now. You are too big a man for me to handle myself. So, now listen to me, if you even look stupid, I'm shooting you. You hear me? If you even twitch, I'm shooting you!"
"You won't have to worry about me, man. I'm cool."

And he was. Craford slept all the way to the airport, and only stirred a time or two on the plane. On the way in from Metro to Police Headquarters he hardly moved. We booked him in a few minutes and Wendy attempted to interview him. After carefully reading him his constitutional rights, she asked if he understood them and he spit out, "You must think I'm crazy to think that anything I say to you *will* be used against me in court. I might be crazy but I ain't no fool."

Wendy looked a little puzzled and then had him escorted to the 9th floor cellblock.

Inspector Barnett tiptoed around for a minute and then quietly asked me, "Any problems?"

"With Wendy? No, she behaved pretty well."

With that, our conversation was over and he walked away.

Wendy's case was decided by a plea bargain and Crawford was convicted of manslaughter. He was sentenced to seven and a half to fifteen years, to be served in the State Prison of Southern Michigan (Jacktown). Wendy felt especially proud that Crawford's arrest became her first homicide conviction.

Chapter Eight: The Death of a Saint

Barbara Hoffman was a wonderful person. Her husband had passed away eleven years earlier and she had the sole responsibility of raising her three children. She had worked as a nurse's aide at Sinai Hospital, in Detroit, for the previous sixteen years. The two boys had grown and moved out, leaving their little sister, Joy Gabrielle, behind with her mother.

Barbara was a Christian lady who had worked in all the nurseries at the church I went to in Detroit. She had also served as an orderly at the church. Barbara was faithful and had a servant's heart . . . and appeared at church as often as her twelve-year-old car would get her there.

There was also a man in her life. He wasn't too interested in church things, but he sure was interested in Barbara. His name was Gregory Tremont.

Joy Gabrielle was only twelve years old when it happened.

***

By 1978, I had become active at my church. The church was located on the east side of Detroit and seated over one thousand people. My place of serving was as an usher in the balcony. Being the parents of four children, my wife and I sat in the balcony where all the other parents with children sat.

The senior usher in the balcony was a man named Robert Lowe. I enjoyed watching him greet folks and take them to their seats. He was a very large man, about forty years of age, and you could tell that he liked what he was doing. He offered his hand and smile to all those who came in. I tried to copy his style and enjoyed working with him. Barbara Hoffman was his sister-in-law. She and Joy Gabrielle usually sat in the balcony too.

It was Christmas of 1981. The holiday had fallen on a Friday and I was privileged to enjoy those days off from work by spending the weekend with my family. I drove to Police Headquarters on Monday and walked down the hall leading to my office. The hallway was strewn with rows of folding chairs, partially emptied Styrofoam coffee cups filled with cigarette butts bobbing like buoys, and more remains of cigarettes on the floor . . . a clear sign of a busy weekend for the working troops. Three male witnesses were trying to make themselves comfortable on the chairs; one was on the floor sleeping with his head resting on a metal seat and the other two with their heads pushed against the plaster walls. The walls had hair-oil stains and these two just added to the assortment.

I had a fresh assignment sitting on my desk awaiting my appearance. I went to our 100-cup coffee pot and poured myself one. It would be the first of ten cups that day. I gave a quick glance at my case and walked out to the hall to see if any of my witnesses were among the three I had walked by. I talked to all three, but none belonged to me. I looked up to find my ushering friend, Robert Lowe, walking toward Homicide. It was a surprise to see him. He had no idea that I was a cop so he was surprised to see me.

"What are you doing here, Jack?" he whispered.

"I work here, Bob. What are you doing here?"

His forehead wrinkled in surprise as he said, "You work in homicide? Well, my sister-in-law, Barb, was murdered and they called me to come down here to identify her or something."

"I'm sorry to hear that, Bob. Did she come to the church?"

He seemed very anxious and was chewing on his lower lip. "Sure, her name is Barbara Hoffman and you would know her, she always sat in the balcony with my niece, Joy Gabrielle, and her friend, Joyce Denton."

As soon as he mentioned Mrs. Denton, I realized that I had seen the three of them at church the weekend prior.

I asked Bob to wait in the hall and told him I would find the detective team that had the case. "I'll be right back."

I checked the Homicide logbook and found that the case was assigned to

Sergeant Carl Freeman and Police Officer Mike Rutter. Carl went by the nickname Lovable, and it wasn't because he was so sweet. He was in his forties but looked much older. He was unmarried, short, and a bit stocky, with his mid-drift overlapping his belt. He seldom smiled and was a chain smoker. It seemed he usually had a long-ash cigarette hanging from his lips and on occasion the ash would fall into his ever present coffee cup. He was addicted to Tums and popped one with every cup of coffee. He assumed he had an ulcer, but feared worse. In spite of his cantankerous, suspicious attitude, he was highly respected as a detective and was usually successful as one. He often questioned me about the changes he'd seen in my life, once I began walking as a believer, and took pleasure in calling me "Christian." He liked to taunt me with, "It ain't gonna last, Christian. I've seen a lot of born-agains come and go." I liked him in spite of his rotten attitude.

"Carl, did you pick up a case on a Barbara Hoffman?"

"Yeah, caught it on Christmas. Santa left her some real coal."

Loveable went out of his way to hide any soft feelings, but I knew he cared and gave every case his best.

"Well, she went to my church. There's a friend of mine in the hall, named Bob Lowe, who was called down for the identification. She was his sister-in-law. He's a good guy, give him the kid-glove treatment."

Carl said that he would. I knew he meant it.

I walked with Carl, introduced him to Bob, and went back to my own case.

My case seemed easy enough. From first appearance, it looked like a justifiable shooting. A hold-up man produced a gun and ordered the owner of the liquor store to turn over the money. The owner produced a gun from under the cash register and three witnesses saw the robber fire three shots, all missing. The storeowner managed to fire two shots at the victim, with one striking him in the throat. He died within a couple of minutes.

I walked over to the Wayne County Morgue, a three-block stroll from

Homicide, to talk with the chief medical examiner, Dr. Wilhelm Shulitz, and to view my victim's body. The hold-up man had an extensive assaultive record. His body was brought out on a gurney and he was stripped of his clothing, leaving him there with nothing but a toe tag. There were several needle marks on his left arm indicating narcotics use. I had his clothing tagged for evidence, blood samples drawn, photos taken, and requested the spent slug to be placed in an evidence tag.

While there, I talked to Dr. Shulitz about the body of Barbara Hoffman. He recalled that she had died a terrible death, one certainly not fitting for a fine Christian lady . . . or anyone else. The cause of death was from blunt-force trauma. She had been beaten to death with a claw hammer. Dr. Shulitz counted nine blows to her skull. He went on to tell me there was much bruising to her arms, indicating that she'd attempted to fend off a blow or two. Even more distressing was evidence of sexual assault. It crossed my mind that she was a person who had lived by the message of love and died by the message of hate. Her body hadn't been claimed yet, so Dr. Shulitz offered to let me see her. I declined. It was difficult enough viewing mangled bodies of people I didn't know. Seeing her would have been more than I needed to see that day.

I left the morgue, walked back to Homicide, and picked up my partner, Cal Noles. We drove out to view the scene of my homicide and after talking to a few neighbors, we went back to headquarters. I brought the shop owner down from the holding cellblock and, after advising him of his constitutional rights, took a written statement from him. Everything pointed to a justifiable homicide and after re-interviewing the witnesses we discharged him.

Tuesday, December 28, 1981

I walked into my office the next day and Loveable was sitting at my desk. He looked anxious to talk to me and was chewing on his nails. With a slight smirk on his face he said, "This Barbara Hoffman was a nice Christian lady, eh?"

"Yeah. What's up?"

"Well, it looks like her live-in boyfriend is the one who killed her."

That was Carl's way of taking a shot at me. In his mind, he had a definition of what a Christian should be, and living together out of wedlock was not part of the bill.

"What's the boyfriend's name?"

"The woman's daughter told us his name is Tree and we found letters to Hoffman from him with the name Gregory Tremont. The girl said that he'd been sleeping over there. Of course, there's nothing wrong with that unless you claim to be a Christian."

I ignored his taunt and said, "Is he in yet?"

"No, but we'll get him. I've got MCMU (the Major Crime Mobile Unit) out looking for him and a couple of the cruiser units. He'll show. We got some smudged prints on the hammer and print traces on some broken glass. The case is coming. We'll get him."

"Thanks, Carl. Let me know when he's in."

"No problem."

I went back to my case and began working on the warrant request. I was satisfied that the case was justifiable and the warrant would be denied as a result of self-defense. It was, and I was relieved for the shop owner. It was just past 1 p.m. when I received a phone call from my seventeen-year-old son, Paul, who was home babysitting the other children during the Christmas break. My wife, Patricia, was in nursing school at the time, and our oldest was in charge of the other three. Apparently, one of them had plugged the upstairs toilet. The water was running over and plaster was falling off the kitchen ceiling. I told him that I would get home as soon as I could.

A short time later, I went to my squad boss, Lieutenant Bob Boisvert, and told him of the problem at home and he excused me. On my way home, I thought about how I was going to kill those kids of mine, but then I began to worry that they might get electrocuted. I began to pray that God would keep them from injury. I guess that could be called a case of mixed emotions.

The mess at home was just short of a disaster. It took every towel in the house to dry things up. However, the plaster wasn't too bad, and none of the kids had drowned or been electrocuted. Three of our kids quickly pointed accusing fingers at the leading suspect, our youngest, Ben, age seven, who had decided to flush two towels into the upstairs toilet.

I called Homicide and talked to my squad boss, Boisvert. He told me to stay home and to enjoy the rest of the day. I thanked him. He told me not to worry and he would keep it in mind that I owed him. I had no idea how soon that debt would come due.

Wednesday, December 29, 1981

It was a cold and cloudy, typical Michigan winter day, when I arrived at Homicide the next morning. I went looking for Loveable and found him by the coffee pot. He informed me they had Tremont in custody and he was keeping his mouth shut. He began shaking his head as he said the case was falling apart. The fingerprints on the hammer were too smudged to be readable and the prints on the glass belonged to the victim. Tremont wouldn't even offer an alibi—he simply wouldn't say anything. There were no witnesses and things were not looking good. He'd been in custody for over eighteen hours and it was at the point of either charging or releasing him. Carl told me he would keep me informed.

I was assigned to help another team of detectives on a different case and was busy the entire day. While I was out, a severe snowstorm hit Detroit, dumping eight to nine inches of snow in a four-hour period. Our crew was over an hour late arriving back to the office. Driving in downtown traffic and fighting the snow had left us beaten and tired. My boss, Bob Boisvert, was sitting at the Homicide desk answering the phones. That assignment was usually considered a punishment detail, and lieutenants rarely stooped to such duty. I asked him why he was there, and he said with a crooked grin on his face, "Rick Nadon called and said he would be an hour or two late getting here because of the snow, so I guess I'm stuck."

The smirk meant that repayment for the toilet incident must not have been far from his mind. Payback can be painful.

"Ah, well, boss, would you like to have me take over for you until Nadon gets in?"

"I think that's a great idea, sergeant. You keep acting like that and you'll make it to heaven someday."

With that, I was nailed to the penalty box.

Detroit was a town of over a million people and with the snowstorm hitting and people cooped up in their homes, we knew that assaults were bound to happen. And at Homicide, we had to be notified whenever someone was injured. The phones were ringing off the hook and there was little time to breathe.

I was vaguely aware that Loveable and Rutter were still working on the Hoffman case.

Around 6 p.m. a drunk staggered up to the desk and asked me if I would take some cigarettes up to a prisoner on the 9th floor. It was a common request and I told him I would when things quieted down.

An hour later, I took the prisoner's elevator to the men's detention area on the 9th floor. I knew all the guards on the floor and told them I was delivering cigarettes to an inmate. I asked if prisoner Tremont was still in custody and they told me where to find him. I dropped the cigarettes off and walked down to see Tremont.

The cell was dark and smelled of urine and cigarette smoke. I could make out a figure sitting on the cot. He said, "What are you looking at?"

"Are you Gregory Tremont?"

It seemed to me that he had a cocky smirk on his face as he said, "Yeah. Who are you?"

"Well, I'm Jack Loshaw, from Homicide. I just wanted to take a look at you. I attend the same church that Barbara went to, and I wanted to see if I recognized you."

He glared at me as he walked toward me at the cell bars.

"Well, do you?"

He had an "up-in-your-face" attitude that many street punks had and crossed his arms across his chest.

I ignored his attitude and said, "No, can't say that I do. You ever been to church with her?"

With that, he seemed to soften as he put his hands in his pockets. "Yeah, one time. It's that big church on the east side."

"Yeah, that's it, Bethesda. Well, listen, I'm not really supposed to be talking to you. You are assigned to two other detectives so I better get going."

It might have been my imagination, or the lighting, but for a moment I saw a glistening in his eyes. The lights were low and it was difficult to see, but I noticed him as he wiped something from his eye.

I took the elevator down, and as I was getting off, Loveable was waiting to board.

He said to me, "I'm going to get Tremont. You want to meet him?"

"I just left him. I think your timing is good. He might be ready to talk. I think he had tears in his eyes."

"Are you kidding? Great!" Loveable jumped on the elevator and was off. I went back to the homicide desk and the phones.

A minute or two later he came down with Tremont. He and his partner, Rutter, went to the interrogation room with the prisoner. A minute later, Rutter came up to the desk.

"Loshaw, we don't know what you saw, but this guy ain't crying. This guy is stone cold. He won't say nothing. We've had him all day and can't get squat out of him. We're gonna have to cut him loose. Can you believe it? This case is going down the tubes. I thought we had him."

I could see the disgust on Rutter's face as he said, "Would you like a crack at him?"

It was rare for a team of detectives to ask another detective to interview their prisoner. It might have been a case of male pride but the truth was it just didn't happen.

"Sure."

I locked my gun in my desk drawer and thought to myself, "If those guys can't break him, what can I do?"

From the Homicide desk to the interrogation room was approximately thirty feet. In those few steps, I had time to pray a simple prayer. "Lord Jesus, please go before me."

It was the only thing I could think to say at the time . . . and there would be many more times in the future that I would offer that same simple prayer.

Seated at a metal desk in the interrogation room was Gregory Tremont. His right hand was handcuffed to an eye-bolt welded to the corner of the desk. I sat down, pulled out some papers, and started right from the beginning. I advised him of his constitutional rights and had him read a section or two of it. My purpose for having the defendant read a line or two was so I could truthfully say in court that I believed he understood his rights, plus I had him read so I felt surer of his understanding of them. I took off his cuff and had him sign it. I felt at ease, I was in my element, and I could tell there was a very special presence in that room. I sensed the Lord was with me and felt sure that good things were going to happen. It was a time I would never forget.

I said nothing special, nothing clever, nothing out of the ordinary. All I said was, "There are always two sides to a story and I would like to hear yours."

Here was Gregory Tremont. A tall, nice-looking, thirty-eight-year-old man, 5'9", 170 pounds, clean shaven, decently dressed man, who now looked very insecure and lost.

From that moment on, he began telling me the details of Barbara Hoffman's murder. He went from being stone cold to very emotional, even sobbing as he related the events.

As a detective, I had seen plenty of phony acts and tears brought on by fear of punishment. This time I truly felt that Tremont had sorrow for Barbara. Although I felt for him, my primary concern was the suffering that she went through. During his confession, I had to suppress the tears that began to well in my eyes. As angry as I felt for what he had done, I had some understanding of his sorrow. He had killed his best friend and was now facing a lifetime of prison.

Taking statements and confessions was considered one of my strengths. I made it a point to make a mistake or two on each page. When the mistake was "discovered," as we re-read the statement, I would have a line drawn through it and the proper word or words written above it. The accused would then place his or her initials at the correction. My purpose was to show that the person giving the statement had, indeed, read the document thoroughly, plus, it drove defense attorneys crazy when they tried to indicate that the statement was from my fanciful imagination.

Gregory Tremont's confession took over two hours and filled two and a half pages. There were times when he sobbed so hard it was hard to understand him. He looked me in the eyes and knew he had hurt me also. I sat there quietly for a few moments and told him I still had a few questions. "Where did you get the hammer from?"

"She bought this sorry Christmas tree that was crooked at the bottom and she hammered some nails in it to keep it straight. It was just laying there."

"Gregory, how many times did you hit her with it?"

"Maybe two times, it happened so quick . . . I didn't know what I was doing."

With that he began crying torrents of tears. I waited for several minutes and then pressed on. He told me in great detail about his anger toward Barbara. He spoke of her being "super spiritual" and how he appreciated her great strength of character, all the while hating her for being so chaste.

After he settled down, I had him initial the mistakes and sign his name on the four pages of his confession. He never admitted to the sexual aspect of the case. I had dealt with a number of rapists and it was not at all unusual for them to ignore or blank-out that part of the crime. I found it curious that a man would readily admit to killing a woman, but be reluctant to talk about raping her. Finally, I said, "In my years on the police department, I have never heard of a husband, or boyfriend, raping and killing the one he loved. Did you have sexual intercourse with her before she died?"

There was no answer.

"Gregory, Sergeant Freeman mentioned to me that you were living with Barbara. Is that true?"

"No, she would let me sleep at her place, maybe four or five times. She told me that we would have to be married before she would let me have sex with her, though. That didn't make no sense, you know?"

"Gregory, did you have sex with her that night?

I was concerned that the rape had happened right after he had killed her and I knew he would never admit to that. It was my way of offering him a respectable way out.

He closed his eyes and was slow in answering. "I don't remember. All I know is I was tryin' to have sex with her on the floor when things got a little out of control. She started hittin' at me and that's when I hit her with the hammer, I guess. I didn't mean to kill her, sergeant. I loved her."

"Do you remember pulling at her pantyhose?"

He closed his eyes again and shifted his feet as he said, "Yeah, I think so. I don't remember. Can we stop this?"

"Sure. Just one more question. Do you think that Barbara is dead because she wouldn't have sex with you?"

He mumbled, "Probably."

At that moment I knew I was dealing with a broken man. He was crying so hard that mucus was pouring out of his nose and mouth. I stood up and put my hand on his shoulder. He looked at me, stood up, and threw his arms around me. I wasn't totally convinced that he was sincere in his grief, so after a few seconds, I told him to be seated and placed the handcuff on his right hand and back through the eye-bolt. I told him to relax for a few moments as I walked out of the room.

It was 9:30 p.m. as I went to the hallway. Loveable and Rutter were pacing the hall like a couple of expectant fathers. Because of all the time I had been with Tremont, they knew I had hit pay dirt. I handed the papers to Carl. "He laid it all out, Carl. She died because of her integrity. She really was a good woman."

Loveable took the papers from me and we shook hands. "Believe it or not, Jack, I'm glad to know she was that kind of person. Thanks for your help, Christian. And I want you to know that I've smoked through a pack of cigarettes waiting on you tonight."

He had that impish smile on his face. I knew that he was sincere.

I was particularly moved by everything that had happened. During my time at Homicide I had taken many confessions, but none like this one. It's my sincere belief that the Lord opened the door so wide for me that a Mack truck could have driven through it. I felt stunned.

Rick Nadon had made it to work and was seated at the homicide desk. I told him I was leaving and I walked the five floors down to the main exit. As I walked down the stairs I covered my mouth, I felt tears coming down my cheeks. Here I was fancying myself as a big tough cop, and my face was now tear-stained.

Barbara and I attended the same church and because of that I felt we were connected. I took it as a great honor that God allowed me to close the case. It was a reward that I could never have expected. I have since learned that God wants to share His glory with those who follow Him and I knew that He was with me that night to make it possible.

As I walked down those five flights of stairs, I began asking myself some questions. "I wonder what God thinks of my job? Sometimes it seems to sink to some very low levels. Sometimes it's a dirty job. And then there are times when I ask if a Christian should even be involved in this kind of work. And once in a while I wonder whether the Lord even cares about me and the things I do. But then I watch as He becomes so small that He enters my little world and, as a result, causes me to look good."

I made it to the first floor of headquarters and walked the three blocks to the mud lot, where I had parked my van. In the spring, the lot was known for swallowing Volkswagens and grown men were seen walking barefoot with mud to their kneecaps. The wonderful parking lot given to Detroit's Finest had sucked their shoes and boots from them. It took some time walking there because of the mounds of snow that night. I started the car and began cleaning it off. All the while, my mind was racing as I considered what had happened. All I did was to ask God to go before me and He had. My heart, mind, and spirit had been touched and all I had done was ask.
After cleaning the van off, my thoughts came back to earth. I couldn't wait to get home to tell my wife, Pat, what had happened. By that time, everyone at church knew of Barbara's death and I needed to talk to someone who would understand. Here was this lady from our church who had been murdered and God allowed me . . . it was too much.

While driving down I-94 on the way home, I remembered a sermon that our pastor had preached when I was a kid. She told about Samson, how he was created for just one thing—to kill Philistines. I'm sure she said a lot of other things but that's the point I remembered. Today I felt that God had saved this Barbara Hoffman case for me.

When I arrived home, the kids were asleep and Pat was in the bathtub. I called to her from the bathroom door and told her what had happened. She asked me to hold on for a second and in a moment the door opened. She was wrapped in a towel. I choked a few times in telling her the story. She hugged me as I told the story and tears fell from her eyes. She told me how proud she was of me and of all that God had done for me that night.

Thursday, December 30, 1981

The next morning, when I walked in to the Homicide Unit, I was greeted with clapping by several of my fellow detectives. Reg Hart was now the Commanding Officer on the Homicide Unit. He and I had worked together for over four years in the Special Assignment Squad when he was a lowly sergeant. He came up to me, put his arm around my shoulder, and said, "I can't tell you how proud I am of you."

"Thanks boss, but we have to talk. Can we go in your office?"

"Sure, Jack. Is everything okay?"

"Yeah. I just need to talk to you privately."

During the years we had worked together, I had learned that Reg had a praying grandmother. She took him to church on a regular basis and he had a decent understanding of godly behavior. He had witnessed the change in my life and liked me. We were friends. We walked into his office, which was decorated with pictures of him being promoted by the Chief and several photos of him with the mayor of Detroit and other political dignitaries. It was an impressive display.

We stood there looking at each other and I looked at the pictures and said, "Well, boss, I've gotta say, you've come a long way from hand-me-down sneakers."

He smiled as he pointed to the photos and said, "This ain't about nothin'. What's up, Jack?"

"Reg, you know me. You know that I'll take the credit when I think it's due. But what happened last night had very little to do with me. I know you know what I'm talking about. All I can tell you is that last night the Lord was with me in that interrogation room. I have never experienced anything like that in my life. All I did was ask Tremont to tell me his side of the story, and he did. Sir, I'm telling you that something very special happened last night and even though I enjoyed the applause today, the credit isn't mine."

Reg stumbled for a moment, "I think I know what you're talking about, Jack. I believe in prayer too, so you keep on praying . . . if that's what it takes."

"Thanks boss for hearing me out. I'll do my part, but it sure is nice to know God does His.

January 1982

The preliminary exam was set for the first Monday in January, 1982, in the 46th District Court in Detroit. The judge was newly appointed James Karlewski, who had been Wayne County assistant prosecuting attorney for seven years. He was highly recognized for his skill and dedication, and had handled two of my homicide cases in the past.

The Gregory Tremont case was Karlewski's first murder exam as a judge. Preliminary exams were often called mini-trials, in which the prosecution was required to offer only enough evidence of guilt to bind the defendant over for trial. Most preliminary hearings took less than a half-hour to conduct.

There were several exams held before mine and by the time my case was called, the courtroom was packed. There were several television and radio reporters present along with two sketch artists intent on drawing pictures of Mr. Tremont. There were three witnesses in our exam, the medical examiner, the identifier, and myself. The defense would certainly want to attack the confession—primarily to see if it was it given freely and voluntarily, or under duress.

When it was my turn to testify, I took the stand and told of the circumstances that brought me into the interrogation room. The Miranda Rights and the confession were read into the record. The defense attorney asked several questions about my qualifications, my methods, and the way I conducted the interview. I noticed that many people in the courtroom seemed genuinely surprised as they learned that I went to the same church as the victim, a black lady. As I testified, I noticed several in the audience edge forward in their seats with eyebrows lifted as I spoke.

The confession was ruled as being proper and introduced into evidence and the case was bound over for trial on the charge of Murder One with an added count of Criminal Sexual Conduct in the first degree.

When the exam was over, I walked out of the courtroom into the hallway. The defense attorney walked over to me and said, "Sergeant Loshaw, your testimony was compelling. I don't mind telling you that I don't understand what happened during your interview with Tremont, but he told you things he won't even tell me. You must have worked some magic on him."

"Counselor, I don't think you would understand how it happened. It wasn't magic in the sense that you know it. Please know this, sometimes the good Lord just steps in and truth comes out."

***

As I have re-examined this case, I've been struck by some strange coincidences. What if my kids had not plugged up the toilet? What if my boss hadn't excused me to go home to take care of it? What if there hadn't been a snow storm that caused the afternoon sergeant to be late? What if Lieutenant Bob Boisvert hadn't been answering phones at the Homicide desk? What if I hadn't offered to replace him? What if the man hadn't asked me to deliver cigarettes to a prisoner? What if I hadn't visited Gregory Tremont in his cell? What if Loveable hadn't been waiting for me at the prisoner elevator? What if Tremont had confessed to the two detectives assigned to him? What if they hadn't asked me to "take a crack at him?" There were too many twists and turns that led me to the interrogation room and as they say, "sometimes God works in mysterious ways." Well, this time He did!

Chapter Nine: Blood and Peckerwood

The streets have to be respected. Just as a good prizefighter works on the body, so do the streets. They grind away slowly until they have drained the strength and the will to continue.

It was the summer of 1980. Chrysler Corporation was in real trouble. Lee Iacocca had just taken over and was busy closing down some of the failing operations, consolidating others, and borrowing money from the federal government in an effort to save the struggling auto giant. He was the hoped for messiah of the Motor City. Cassie Thompson worked for Chrysler.

Cassie was a twenty-two years old when it happened. She was one of the top graduates of Finney High School in Detroit. She went to Wayne State University and earned a bachelor's degree in business administration. She was hired by the Chrysler Corporation and worked with computers. After only six months she received a promotion. Coupled with the good news was the fact that she was being transferred to Newark, New Jersey. Detroit was all that she knew and she didn't want to leave. Some people actually enjoyed living in Detroit and Cassie was one of them.

Cassie was slim and only stood five foot two inches tall. She was a beautiful girl who loved to dance and socialize. When she went dancing, she was known to always wear a butterfly that was painted below her left eye. I was told she had one of those smiles that would light up a room. She was her daddy's pride and joy.

On the dance floor, the fellas called her "Cutesy Cassie." Besides being very attractive, she was also tough. Lots of Detroit kids were that way and it was said of her, "she didn't take no stuff." Cassie had fought her way up the ladder to her position at Chrysler and tragically it was this same quality that brought about her death.

***

Red Rooster's lounge was located on Livernois Avenue just south of the John

C. Lodge Expressway. On a good night it was not unusual for crowds of two to three hundred people to pack the place. The dance floor was raised three feet off the floor and could accommodate thirty gyrating couples. However, when a slow dance was played, the number of dancers would increase two fold. The proprietor, C. J. Hedgewood, was a grizzled old gent who grew up with the mayor of Detroit, Coleman A. Young.

It had been decided that the Red Rooster would be a good place to have a going away party for Cassie. Even though she was the guest of honor that night, only a few people knew who she was or what she was about. Her escort was a robust young man of approximately three hundred pounds who went by the unlikely name of "Big Daddy Romance." Big Daddy pretended to be a pimp with a stable of girls, but the truth was, in spite of his menacing size and grumpy demeanor, he had no heart for the streets and fooled no one. In order to make up for his lack of heart, he always carried a .38 pistol, which he kept tucked in the waistband of his ample tummy.

It was 10 p.m. when Big Daddy picked Cassie up at her home and drove her to the club in his beat-up 1971 Buick deuce and a quarter (225). He didn't have any spare change so he bypassed the valets and parked the car himself. The plan was to party until closing time and then adjourn to an after-hours joint. In the Motor City, white folks called those places blind pigs, but in the black community there were always referred to as after-hours joints. The name of this local blind pig was called Al Kaline's. I'm sure this Hall of Fame right fielder would have dropped his jock strap had he known.

It was just after 1 a.m., Cassie had danced with several partners, and more were eagerly waiting. She finished a dance with a young man named Barry Wooten. They were just dance partners and didn't know each other's last names. From all accounts, Cassie, with her white blouse, short red skirt, and painted butterfly tattoo, was not only the prettiest girl in the house, but also the best dancer. She had lots of dance partners that night. She usually did.

While Cassie danced, a dangerous looking man entered the bar and walked close to where she was. He stood at the dance rail and remained on the main deck. He looked taller than his actual height of 5'11" and was very muscular. He wore a red tank–top shirt, which displayed large biceps and a washboard stomach. His physique was the result of doing hundreds of pushups a day and lifting weights by the hour. Years in prison allowed for plenty of time to work on one's body.

He looked to be about thirty years old and had very short hair, which was unusual in those days of the Afro. Several people remarked later that his eyes were gray and looked very scary and unnatural. He used his body and scary eyes to intimidate people. He enjoyed staring and draining the courage from anyone foolish enough to stare back. He had practiced that art for hours while glaring at the cement blocks of his prison cell. He always felt exhilarated about being good at staring at and scaring people.

On that night the music was particularly loud, partly due to the size of the crowd, and also because the disc jockey was practically deaf. The man with the scary eyes said something to Cassie. She either didn't hear or simply chose to ignore him. Regardless, the man, who was not very patient in the first place, pushed the conversation. He reached over the dance rail with both hands, squeezed Cassie's buttocks and as one witness stated, "Not flirting like, but real mean like." She whirled around and instinctively slapped his face. She was feisty. Her partner, Barry Wooten, in a moment of gallantry, stepped between Cassie and the gray-eyed man. Some vile words came spewing out of the mouth of the molester and Wooten quickly backed off. When the music finished, the couple came off the dance floor and walked toward the bar. The dangerous looking man with the grey eyes appeared again and grabbed Cassie's breast. She reached for a bottle from the bar and tried to swing it, but in an instant her attacker seized her wrist, bottle and all. With his free hand he unzipped the little black bag he carried on his shoulder, pulled out a small black gun, put it to Cassie's face and in the darkness of the lounge a bullet exploded.

Before walking out of the lounge, the shooter slowly and deliberately looked around the room with those scary eyes, and with the gun still in his hand and said, "Now, does anyone else want some of this?"

Getting no replies, he nonchalantly placed his pistol back into his shoulder purse and strolled outside into the night air.

Cassie had fallen against the bar and slid down into a crouched position. Her pretty red skirt was pushed upward exposing her underwear to all those who cared to look. In panic, she stood up with her hands clutching her throat and stumbled through the crowd, desperately trying to pull air into her lungs. Huge amounts of blood were pouring out of her cheek and neck area as she finally made her way through the maze of people and out into the street. Here she again collapsed, falling next to the street curb. She was dead. Twenty-two years old. Intelligent. Pretty. A bright future ahead wasted. Now, she was Homicide file 80-344. She was the three hundredth and forty-fourth homicide victim of 1980, and there would be many more. Her case was assigned to Sergeants Loshaw and Noles.

The Scene

It was just before 2 a.m. when my phone rang. My loving boss Inspector Ross Barnett was on the other end.

"Jack?"

"Yeah. What time is it?"

"Don't worry about that, crime-fighter. We've got a bad one. Pack your six-shooter and get your narrow butt movin'. I need you to go over to Livernois and the freeway. I'll have the techs meet you there. It's a bar killin' and we got a dead girl at the scene. Get your scene investigation done as quickly as you can 'cause we're gonna need you down here. We got a million witnesses on the way to Homicide. Oh, by the way, did you get a good night's sleep?"

It was Sunday morning. Most normal people went to church with their families on Sunday. Not me. I went to murder scene investigations. Secretly though, I had to admit that in many ways homicide scenes had become spiritual experiences for me.

The scene was simple enough. Her body was just outside the bar entrance, lying in a heap, face up, with empty eyes staring at the night sky. Blood was caked on her hair, dark stains covered her white blouse, and there was a small ugly entrance wound below the butterfly tattoo on her left cheek. An elongated wound was found below her chin. It was the point of exit. From the amount of blood and the gaping exit wound it was clear that she had died quickly. It was also clear that she was just a kid and even in death she was still a pretty girl.

I had the evidence technicians take photos of the victim, the outside and inside of the building, and sketches of the scene. The search for the expended slug began at the sight of the largest amount of blood where Cassie had fallen at the bar. The technician, Rich Nadon, crawled along the floor and gave out a yell when he came across the slug.

"I've got it boss, not too damaged and looks like a .38 caliber."

I had him take photos of the slug and he put it in a folder with an evidence tag on it. We continued the search to see if more than one bullet was fired and to look for an expended shell casing in case it had been fired by an automatic pistol. Nadon then collected blood samples, tagged them, and we were finished with the scene.

The Witnesses

After processing the scene, I drove down to 1300 Beaubien, Police Headquarters. The Homicide Section was located on the fifth floor and there were two uniformed police officers watching over approximately thirty-five witnesses who were seated in the folding metal chairs that adorned the hallway. As was usual in most homicide cases, very few people wanted to be involved. Most of the witnesses denied being there, let alone seeing or hearing anything. And we knew that many had fled the scene when they saw what had occurred. Of the group, a large number of reluctant witnesses claimed to have been in the restroom at the time of the shooting. The evidence tech and I had examined both restrooms. Full capacity would have allowed five occupants so I knew most were lying.

After interviewing the witnesses, six people admitted to seeing the murder: Barry Wooten (her dance partner), Johnnie Davis (the disc jockey), Karen

Williams, Latisha Feltrin, Pristine Jenkins (all friends of Cassie), and Big Daddy Romance (aka Daniel Moncrief). None of the witnesses admitted knowing the name of the killer.

I spent over four hours interviewing the witnesses. I had photos taken of the witnesses. Before they were released and driven back to their cars at the scene, I had photos taken of them. The photos would refresh my memory if I went searching for them.

The Wayne County Morgue

I released the witnesses just before 9 a.m.. Then I walked the three blocks to the morgue at Monroe and Brush streets. It was a two story, plain brick building, likely built in the 1920s, that housed the Medical Examiner and his attendants, most of whom spoke little English.

The building had a peculiar, unforgettable, and indescribable odor. Bleach was used to try to cover the odor, but somehow decaying flesh and formaldehyde managed to seep through every room. Most cops did all they could to stay away from the place, and most referred to it as the "Butcher Shop" It was here that human bodies were cut open with what was called the Y incision. The less sensitive in the force called it "making a canoe." To many of the less enlightened, it seemed barbaric, and many prospective homicide detectives transferred to other detective duties rather than having to stand watching an autopsy.

The head forensic pathologist was the renowned Dr. Wilhelm Shulitz. He was a man who was fully committed to his work. Dr. Shulitz enjoyed talking to me and he liked most police officers. He loved to teach, and as he performed an external examination of the bodies, he would explain to all what he was seeing and then translate it into his medical opinion. Whenever he was asked a question his eyes would sparkle and then, in his heavy German accent, he would go to great lengths to answer. He was especially savvy when it came to testifying in court, which he did thousands of times, and he relished the opportunity to teach everyone with his expertise. Dr. Shulitz came alive as he taught judges, attorneys, jurors, witnesses, and even defendants. His eyes often penetrated the defense table as he explained the suffering victims went through on their way to eternity. His medical credentials were more than impressive and defense attorneys gladly waived the reading of them.

I walked through the morgue waiting room and spoke to two of the clerks. It had been a busy night in Motown with three homicides, two fatal overdoses, one suicide, and two killed in a car accident. Two of the waiting room chairs were occupied by men called in to identify loved ones. Their eyes were reddened. I was curious to know if one was Cassie's father.

I walked into the morgue viewing room. An attendant brought Cassie Thompson's body out on a metal gurney. One of the wheels was flopping around, making the cart dogtrot as it was pushed it into the viewing area. Waiting in the viewing area were four doctors, all of foreign descent and with names that were hard to pronounce. They worked under Dr. Shulitz. The white bed sheet was pulled from Cassie's body and the doctors quickly examined the wound to her face and the injury to her neck. Dr. Shulitz asked me if this was my case. I nodded and I began to tell him what I knew at that point.

It was noted that Miss Thompson was a well-nourished, twenty-two-year-old black female, five foot two inches tall, and weighing one hundred and twelve pounds. She was still wearing the red skirt and white blouse, which were now saturated with a dark stain that we all knew was blood. Her panty hose were still on and her shoes were on the rack below the metal stretcher. There were no injuries to the legs, torso, hands, or arms. Her hands were covered with dried blood. There was an ugly dark spot of gunpowder residue buried just below her left eye at the cheekbone. This was quickly determined to be the entry wound. Her clothing was removed and there were no other signs of trauma. The doctors checked her arms and they were without visible signs of narcotics use.

Cassie Thompson lay there dead and naked except for the tag wrapped with wire around her right big toe. Her clothing had been placed in a brown paper bag, just like those at grocery stores, and given to me. Blood samples were taken to test for alcohol levels. Dr. Shulitz asked me if I needed anything else and I requested fingernail scrapings and hair samples. It was better to have too much evidence than not enough.

In a short time, the body was taken to the basement operating room where the autopsies took place. The medical examiner determined that Miss Thompson had died from a near-contact wound to the head, by a projectile splintering the cheekbone and glancing downward like a perverted pinball which exited through her larynx. If her life hadn't been stilled her voice most certainly would have been.

Spencer Thompson, Cassie's father, was a short, slightly built man in his mid-forties. He was Cassie's father and was seated in the visitors' room waiting to identify his daughter's body. She was his only child. He had worked at the Chrysler Assembly Plant for the last twenty-one years. His wife had run off with a fellow worker shortly after Cassie's birth and never reappeared. He had raised her by himself with the aid of his mother.

Mr. Thompson had been notified of his daughter's death by telephone just after 6 a.m. It was now near 10:30 a.m. and he still hadn't seen her. He had suffered the extreme anguish of waking to the news of his daughter's murder. He dressed in a fog and called a friend to drive him to the morgue. As I stood there ready to talk to him, a clerk directed Cassie's father to a black and white television. It was through the TV screen that he would be asked to identify his daughter's body. The blood on her face had been washed away and a white towel was placed around her blood soaked hair. When she appeared on the TV screen, he let out a long low moan.

He had hoped to be able to touch his little girl, he wanted to talk to her, to cry over her. All he was allowed to do was to view her image on an eighteen-inch black and white screen.

The clerk said, "Is that Cassie Thompson?"

He sobbed quietly and said, "Yes, she's my daughter."

His grief was deep, but there were forms that "just had to be signed." So, to add to the indignity of which Mr. Thompson had already suffered, some papers were shoved in front of him along with a ballpoint pen and an X was placed where he was expected to sign. The callous and impersonal act of placing an X at the appropriate spot was equivalent to saying, "In case you're too dumb to read this stuff at least you'll be able to scrawl your name next to it."

Mr. Thompson signed the document without a word of protest. Unlike his daughter, he was not a fighter or a complainer. He just did what he was supposed to do.

I told his driver that I would make sure that Mr. Thompson was given a ride home. I invited him to walk with me a block to Greektown where we stopped for coffee and a roll. We talked as one father to another and in many ways, I could feel his sorrow. He talked about raising her as an infant to her going to school to attending Wayne State University, and finally the good job at Chrysler. He asked the question over and over again, "Why would someone kill Cassie?"

I told him that we would do everything possible to find the man who did it and if there was a reason I would let him know. This case, like the streets, had taken a devastating toll on Spencer Thompson and seeing his sorrow was eating at my soul. I told him that I would stay in touch, gave him my card, and told him to call me with any questions. I had him sign nothing.

We walked back to my car and I drove him home. When I returned to my office I began reviewing the witness statements. Central Photo had developed the scene photos and I looked at each one carefully. There really was not much to see—some poor kid with a promising future destroyed, now just another homicide number.

Back to Basics and a Break

I decided to go back to the scene. It was now broad daylight and I hoped to see or find something that we might have missed earlier that night. My partner, Cal Noles and I drove to the lounge, which was locked, so we walked around the parking lot, kicked a few cans in the alley, and talked to a few business owners in the area. No one would admit to having seen anyone who looked like the man with the gray eyes in their shops. There was nothing new and all we had to go on was the description of the killer.

Because of the connection between Chrysler Corporation and a young Detroiter being killed, two newspapers, *The Detroit News* and *The Detroit Free Press* ran big stories on the incident. Their articles would provide many tips, mostly from those wishing to collect the $2,000 secret witness voucher provided by the newspapers. Of the many calls that came in, most were of little value. Finally, six days later on Friday, something of value came in. The phone call was sent to me and it sounded like an older black man's voice.

"You the detective on that case 'bout that Chrysler girl gittin' kilt?"

I told him I was and he said, "The dude who kilt the girl is named Blood and he ain't been out of the joint but a few months. He's the same dude who kilt the people back in March when he jest got out, ya' know. Yeah, like I said, he should not have hurt that girl."

I asked him, "So how do you know that Blood killed the girl?"

"Now, listen up Screw, we about done talkin' ya' understand? You all ain't g'tting no more phone calls, this is it. The peoples he kilt back in March was up on the freeway and he got paid good for doin' it. Now, that's it."

The phone went dead. I knew from him calling me Screw that he must have known Blood while serving time with him in prison, as that was the term used to identify the prison guards. This wasn't the typical phone call looking for a reward. This man had something to say and I hoped it made sense. He had sounded very jumpy and wanted to end the conversation quickly, likely thinking the call could be traced. Of course, we had no such technology at that time. I hoped he would call back, but I knew the chances were slim.

I pulled out the homicide logbook for March and discovered there had been two people murdered on the freeway that month. They were found in a car at the side of an overpass on the John C. Lodge Freeway near Southfield Road. It had all the signs of a contract hit. The man had been shot-gunned in the face and thrown into the backseat. His female companion had suffered the same fate, however, she was stuffed into the trunk with the deck lid was partially opened, and her leg sticking out. It appeared that whoever had killed them was pleased to advertise what had been done and wanted their bodies to be discovered. It seemed the murders had taken place at another location and the killer had taken them to the freeway. He likely had another car follow him. The car containing the victims was a 1976 Cadillac El Dorado, or as the people on the street called it, an "El Dora Doo." The case was assigned to members of Squad Seven who specialized in dope killings.

I went through the file and looked for the name Blood and found nothing. Then I read all the witness statements and again found nothing relating to the man with the scary eyes. I walked into Squad Seven and talked to an old friend and the lead investigator, Myron Durecki. He was a tenacious detective and didn't miss much. He was a street-wise detectives who seldom had to raise his voice to get his message across to the street folks. He gave me a quick rundown of the events and suspects and said, "Jack, the name Blood never came up in our case and I don't recall anyone speaking of anyone with that description."

"Well Myron, if you hear of anyone matching his description let me know."

"No problem. I will get his name out on the street and see what happens."

"Is there any life in your case?"

"No, Jack, we turned a lot of stuff over to Narcotics that helped them, but this case is almost six months old and I've got nowhere to go with it."

"I know where you're at, been there, and it ain't fun. If I get anywhere with mine I will keep you up to date. Who knows, there could be a tie-in."

"Thanks, Jack and good luck."

The Identification Section was located on the fourth floor of headquarters, one story below homicide. They had a fairly extensive nickname section and to my surprise I found over three hundred Blood's on file. Of the group, fifteen or so had the same relative physical description as my killer. A couple of them could indeed pass for looking scary, and a few even looked menacing.

I traced down four of the Bloods during my shift and felt certain they were clear, three being in jail and the other having died in a street shooting two years before Cassie's death. I had the five good witnesses brought to Homicide to view the rest of the mug photos. All were quick in deciding that the killer wasn't among them. It was becoming clear that an easy identification of the suspect didn't looking promising.

The lab results started coming in. The lead projectile found at the scene was a .38 caliber slug fired from a revolver. The markings on an expended bullet are much like fingerprints. No gun will mark the lead like another one. Each is unique in leaving what are called lands and grooves on the lead. A firearms expert can testify with scientific certainty that a particular gun fired a particular bullet. Judges and juries like that sort of thing. Sometimes a microscope can be a powerful tool in a criminal case. This particular bullet was held on an evidence tag and officially listed as a .38 special with six lands and grooves, left twist lubaloy bullet.

I had learned through experience that murder weapons were often destroyed, buried, or tossed into the Detroit River, but every once in a while it would be held onto by the killer. Sometimes they were sold or simply passed along. In the latter cases, all that had to be done was to backtrack the ownership to the guilty party. It sounded simple enough, eh?

I updated the teletype on my wanted man by adding the information that he was armed with a .38 caliber revolver. I also notified the gun lab to apprise me whenever they tested a .38 revolver. In Detroit, hundreds of guns were confiscated monthly so the lab people were not too pleased with my request. The department's firearm experts never tested the vast majority and the only ones given that sort of priority treatment were those that were likely to end up in court. The thought crossed my mind that many murder weapons were never tested because someone failed to do the right thing, such as tagging the gun properly as to caliber, or someone tossed it into the wrong storage bin. I had images of my murder weapon being sent over to the Ford Rouge Smelting Plant where it would be melted down to become part of a rear bumper on a Mustang.

***

The Streets are always calling . . . beckoning . . . enticing . . . tempting to the eye and ear . . . offering promises that can't be kept.

I went through every unsolved homicide file since the double murders in March. I could find nothing that came close to matching the man with the gray eyes. It was tedious and boring. Soon the scientific results, toxicology, came in from the morgue. It showed that Cassie Thompson's blood, type B, contained a blood alcohol content of .06 percent. In Michigan, .10 percent blood alcohol content was enough to be declared legally drunk, and at .07 it was considered too high for the operation of an automobile. This fact supported what the witnesses had said. Cassie was more interested in dancing and talking than she was in drinking.

That bit of information could become important in the event that the killer's attorney suggested that the victim was the instigator of her own alcohol-induced tragedy. I had been in court often enough to recognize that many defense attorneys were not warm-blooded creatures and many were willing to stoop to unimaginable levels to win the release of their clients. It was pleasing to find that Cassie was fairly sober rather than fairly drunk. Lastly, the report mentioned that there were no traces of narcotic substances found in her blood.

Most cases are solved in the first twenty-four to forty-eight hours and I was already in my fifth day. We had been hit with a rash of homicides after her death and I was worried that my loving boss, Ross Barnett, might throw another assignment on my desk so I would be further behind the proverbial eight ball. Thankfully, he didn't. I continued to work on the routine aspects, re-read all the statements and re-interviewed the witnesses. I talked with each officer who responded to the scene and examined each piece of evidence. It was all standard stuff, boring stuff, and certainly not the stuff from which movies are made.

I began having the various men with the nickname Blood brought in. I soon became weary of talking to all of those supposedly dangerous looking men with scary eyes. Most of them could not hold a stare for more than five seconds. I appreciated the street *coppers* bringing the suspects down to Homicide, even though I was getting no closer to finding the killer. I was afraid he was still out there loose on the streets just "starin' and scarin'" people. All I could hope for was that he wasn't out there killing another Cassie.

One of the more interesting Bloods brought to me was a handsome young man named Tyrone T. Bloodworth. A man with below average intelligence, he was the right age. Thirty. The right weight. Stood five-foot eleven. He had a large afro parted in the middle, and had scary eyes. Actually, one of his eyes was made of glass and I found it difficult talking to him not knowing which one was real and the other artificial. Because of his disability, one could say that he had a scary eye. During my questioning of him, I found myself staring at the glass eye several times. Bloodworth was a small-time thief and admitted to doing some bad things, but denied killing anyone. Being interviewed by a real detective was one of the highlights of his life. He was ready to confess to just about anything, including the missing Mr. Hoffa, but denied any involvement in the death of Miss Thompson.

"Man, I don't even have no gun, and if I did I sho' 'nuff couldn't shoot it straight. You gotta believe me I ain't killed nobody."

He was released after thirty minutes of conversation.

The Boss

On September 7th, it rained all day. No one wanted to go out into the streets to get soaked and many detectives found inside work to do. Rain was like a plague to many cops and in many ways it was like being quarantined. I thought about the high suicide rates in places like Seattle and other areas of the Great Northwest. I could understand the reason because ugly clouds and rain produce some ugly thoughts.

Inspector Ross Barnett called me into his office. Being called into his office was one of the things most hated by homicide guys. First of all, it was raining, and second of all, I didn't want to see lightning coming from him. He wanted to know the status of my investigation.

Barnett was a career officer. He joined the department in 1946 immediately after the war ended. He never talked about himself, but rumors abounded that he was right next to John Wayne when they invaded Normandy. He was certainly the toughest, meanest, most ornery man I had ever met. I liked and feared him. He was intimidating in size, being 6'3", 250 pounds, with a full head of gray wiry hair, a gravely booming voice, and dark eyes that wouldn't accept cowardice. He could spot a hypocrite in a minute. A two-inch scar on his chin marked his face. One of the more reckless detectives said that Barnett's reddish face was the result of spending too many nights drinking at the Athens Bar and screaming profanities at some less-than-ambitious detectives.

In some ways, he reminded me of my father. I feared my father because he was the one who administered discipline. And that same fear that kept me on the straight and narrow was what gave me peace at night. I knew that if anyone came into our home, they would have to deal with him first, and I knew he was no one to mess with. So fear was coupled with peace and I felt the same way about my boss.

Eight years into his career, his partner was shot down. The perpetrator was chased down by Barnett and in exchange of gunfire the criminal suffered seven gunshot wounds, leaving him dead at the scene. An interesting note, tucked away in the shooting report, was that Barnett was carrying a six shot revolver. The question has always remained, "one for good measure?"

He seldom smiled. On those few occasions when he did, it was only with those he felt most comfortable, and then he seemed boyishly bashful about it. It was almost as if he had to apologize for smiling. Ross Barnett was also the hardest working man I had ever met. He had the ability to work for twenty-four straight hours, take an hour nap, and go back at it for another twelve hours. He was tough. He wouldn't quit and made it very clear that he didn't like quitters. In his mind, every case was solvable. To all those who were into new technology he often snorted, "Shoe leather, sweat, and guts are the answer." He was from the old school and it worked. It seemed to me that no killer was smart enough to fool him and lazy detectives weren't tolerated. Another thing that appealed to us was that he *despised* the FBI guys. He once told their lead investigator from the Detroit office that he would be lucky if he could find his butt with both hands.

It seemed that Barnett had a special instinct; he could smell fear and weakness. He was so intimidating in his mannerisms and speech that many of the tough Detroit Dudes would admit to almost anything just to be free of him. The strength of his character was awesome and the rest of us fed off him. He drove us as the way Vince Lombardi did his Packers or Bobby Knight his Hoosiers. He didn't love any of us, but would not allow anyone else to ever chew us out. He was often outranked, but none of us ever saw him outdone by any superior. We knew what they feared. We knew . . . they feared him.

One evening a Detroit Police Officer went off the deep end. In a tragic moment, the officer killed his wife and two children. The last child hid herself under a coffee table before her father shot her. It was a terribly senseless crime. The responding officers found the assailant sitting at the curb outside his home in a catatonic state. A District Deputy Chief, one of the top five positions in the department, was summoned to the scene. He and the killer came down to homicide and walked into Barnett's office. The Chief had his arm around the defendant and stated, "He's been through a heck of a lot and I want him treated right."

I was out in the hall and I saw Barnett's face redden, his jaw tighten, and veins bulge on his temple area as he stood up and walked out from behind his desk. The chief and the prisoner began to back out from his office when Barnett said, "This man will be treated like any other heartless coward who just killed his wife and kids, so if you'll stop kissing him to death and get your dead carcass out of my office I will have one of *my* men deal with him."

The chief seemed speechless and raised his hands as he walked out to the hallway. Barnett called to my partner, Cal Noles, who took the accused into the interrogation room and advised him of his constitutional rights. Amazingly his catatonia disappeared and he managed to communicate enough to request a lawyer.

So on that day when I was called into Barnett's office, as usual, he wasn't smiling. He questioned me as to covering the basics of Cassie's death and advised me not to place too much emphasis on the anonymous tip concerning Blood. With that, he encouraged me, as only he could do, to go out and catch the killer. "Don't sit around here talking to every Blood in town. Get out on Livernois, knock on doors, and find this guy."

Barnett had a way of making me feel nervous and I knew I could never fool him so I didn't try. I feared him enough that I would never lie to him, because I had seen other men fudge the truth around him and to do so could result in their premature deaths. We often accused him of having a built in lie detector. All during the time I worked for him, I believe he gave me one compliment . . . but it might have been my imagination.

I was so inspired after my "conversation" with Barnett that I started hammering at the Bloods again. Someone was going to pay for me having an office meeting with my boss. I had several brought in and tormented them with my questions, but when the day was over I was still looking for the man with the scary eyes.

The Break

The following day I walked across the street to the Wayne County Jail. It was one of those old buildings, with an inscription carved into the masonry. It simple read, COVNTY JAIL. It never made much sense to me that the old-timers couldn't make the letter "U" so they did the next best thing and replaced it with a "V," making it practically un-pronounceable.

I went to the clerk's office and asked to see the records of all inmates who were discharged within the first three months of the year. None of them had a name that I could remotely connect with the name Blood. I then talked with a few of the deputies, each of whom could tell me about some real bad dudes who were recently released, but none could come up with a Blood.

I walked back to my office and started making phone calls to various police detention centers. One of the calls I placed was to the State Prison of Southern Michigan, which was located in the nice rural town of Jackson, Michigan. Practically everyone referred to the place as Jacktown. The gentleman receiving my call acted about as interested in answering my questions as he was doing a three to ten year term in the slammer. He mentioned that several dozen Bloods had come and gone during his tenure and couldn't recall any of them having gray, scary eyes.

I spent the rest of the day on the phone calling most of the correctional facilities in the state. By the time I had made my seventh call, I had my speech memorized.

"Hi, my name is Jack Loshaw. I work in Detroit homicide and I want to know if you had a man released during the first part of the year that went by the name Blood?"

It appeared that everyone I talked to seemed uninterested and bored. I was quickly losing hope in what was likely a futile effort. My next call was to Marquette State Prison in the Upper Peninsula. The Upper is over three hundred miles from downtown Detroit and is separated by the Straits of Mackinaw. The shortest route from the lower to the Upper Peninsula is over the Big Mac, which is the world's largest suspension bridge. The city of Marquette is another 260 miles from that bridge. It is also a few light years away from the crime and deprivation of Detroit. I had been there on two work-related occasions and after tromping through sixteen inches of snow in October I decided never to return again, unless at gunpoint.

A gruff sounding man answered the phone. He identified himself as Odell Chauncey. I again repeated my spiel about how I knew it was a long shot, but I was wondering if, by any chance, he might have remembered a real bad actor by the name of Blood who had been discharged earlier in the year.

"Yeah, I know Blood. Do I know Blood? He was the baddest of the baddest. He was here a long time. When he first got here he was known as Youngblood, and was nothin' but a boy. He was here so long that they dropped the Young. He was tough and mean. I mean to tell you he was *too* young to be so mean. Everyone here knew him or, at least, knew of him. He done more than ten years here, and mostly in solitary. Every time that dude got out of the hole someone got hurt and hurt bad. Everyone knew it was Blood doin' the hurtin', but findin' witnesses against him wasn't 'bout to happen.

"Let me put it this way, I ain't sure that I'd even snitch on him cuz that sucker would sho' 'nuff find a way to get ya', know what I mean?"

"Mr. Chauncey, do you know his real name or his prison number?"

"Oh, yeah. It was Dawson. Marshall Dawson. He was one tough bugger. Had those gray eyes, you know. Spent most of his time in the hole, like I said. We got some mean folks in here, including the guards, and I don't know of anyone who wanted to mess with him. He wasn't even that big . . . only went about two hundred pounds and was maybe five foot eleven or so."

As soon as Mr. Chauncey took a breath I told him, "He sounds like the guy I'm after."

Chauncey jumped in, "He done killed someone didn't he?"

"Yeah. He killed a girl in the case I'm working on and probably a couple of other people back in March."

"Makes sense to me. He got out of here, let's see . . . March 17. He's got people in Detroit. Sure don't surprise old Odell none. He is one bad mutha."

"What was he in for, Odell?"

"Well, he was shipped to us from Jacktown. They got tired of his act so they sent him to us. Word was that he was involved in a killing down y'all way and he got sent for somethin' like ten to twenty-five. But I know for a sure fact that he did almost eight years in solitary up here. He was dangerous and I don't mind telling you that I ain't been missin' him. When you get your hands on him, be careful . . . he is one seriously bad dude."

"Odell, I just want to thank you. And mister, I want you to know that you are going to heaven!"

"That ain't a bad deal for just givin' you that info. You have a good day sir, and I hope you catch him and make sure you watch your fanny, 'cuz I ain't kiddin' . . . he's a bad one. And please don't send him back up here."

When I hung up the phone my ear was hurting. I knew that Odell would have been pleased to rattle on for hours about Blood, but I had reached an adrenaline high and couldn't wait to start digging into Marshall Dawson's name. I literally ran down the flight of stairs to the Identification Section and pulled the file on Dawson. My heart was pounding and I realized again the reason I loved working in homicide. His file was not very thick, which made sense as I discovered he had been convicted and sent away when he was eighteen years old. The reports showed that he was the driver of a stickup team who went into a Cunningham's Drug Store, robbed the place, and shot the clerk to death. He and his crew were arrested and brought to trial, with Dawson being sentenced to serve eight to fifteen years. For him to spend any time past the minimum of eight years meant that he had been a correctional problem in prison. There was a thirteen-year-old black and white mug shot of him in his jacket and his eyes jumped right off the picture. His eyes, even in black and white, had an unusual look to them . . . *they looked scary.*

I took the photo, made copies of his file, and ran down to Central Photo to have twenty copies made of his mug shot.

My heart was pounding and I didn't have the patience to wait for the elevator, so I raced up the five flights to my office and told Cal all that had happened. He popped a couple of Tic Tacs in his mouth, trying to cover up the odor of ten-hour-old coffee. His face came alive as he said, "Let's get some guys and go get him."

I called down the hall to the Major Crimes Mobil Unit (MCMU). That unit was usually stocked with some of the finest street policemen in the department. The men there loved going out on raids, kicking in doors, and ridding the populace of bad guys. Two of them walked down the hall and into my office. I filled them in on my case and on Mr. Dawson. Even though his last known

116

address was from 1968, we decided to make the place. After all, it was only six o'clock.

His address was in a lovely part of town known to cops as The Bowels. The wonderful mayor of Detroit, who often referred to himself as the HMFIC (head mother f---er in charge), hadn't quite gotten around to beautifying the area, but as he told his constituency, it was on the agenda. The dwelling looked like it had been cared for, which surprised me. Most of the windows were unbroken and the metal grate on the front door looked less than twenty years old. One of the men from MCMU and I took the front door and Cal and the other officer went to the back. I banged on the door and twenty seconds later a sleepy-eyed older man opened the front door.

I asked him his name and he said, "Dawson. You lookin' for Marsh?"

"Yes, is he home?"

"Nah, he ain't been home for three days and that's all right with me. What's he done?"

Cal came around from the back and I said to Dawson, "You mind if we come in and look around?"

"Yeah, I mean no. Come on in, but like I tolt you, he ain't here."

We walked in and the place was fairly well kept. We checked the rooms but there was no one there except Mr. Dawson and a few crawly things. At the end of the hallway was a room that Mr. Dawson said belonged to Marshall. It had an eyebolt in the door frame and was padlocked.

"You got a key for this lock?"

"You kiddin'? Marsh don't trust nobody and that includes me."

"Do we have permission to go in, or do we have to get a search warrant?"

"I don't care what you do, just don't wreck my door."

I told him that we'd be careful and, if needed, we would have city carpenters come out and fix any damage. It only took a couple of shoulder hits to pull the eyebolt out and we were in.

The room was quite neat, being cleaner than the rest of the house. The bed was made and the closet had a couple of shirts, a few pair of jeans, and six pairs of shoes. Marshall was no clothes hound. Taped to the wall at the head of the bed were several Polaroid photographs. Most of them were of the obscene nature, with Marshall posing with some very immodest women. I was pleased that Cassie Thompson was not one of them. Two of the photos were of Marshall holding an automatic pistol in his right hand and approximately twelve one-hundred dollar bills in his left. The money was fanned out like playing cards. I thought to myself, "Aren't photographs a wonderful way to capture those special memories?"

I peeled off those pieces of memorabilia and put them in my sport coat pocket. We now had current photos of the man with the scary eyes.

Cal was on his hands and knees looking under the bed and came out with a bulletproof vest. In the movies bad guys are seen wearing vests, but in my career I had never come across anyone who wore or owned one. Marshall was the first, and I was becoming convinced that he was a real Motown gangster.

"Marshall's your son, right? Well, where is he?"

"Oh yes, he's my son, but we ain't tight. Tell the truth I don't want to be tight with him."

It was at that time I was thinking that Marshall had probably forgotten to send his dear old dad a few Father's Day cards.

"When are you expecting him back?"

"I'm not. Least I hope he don't come back. He ain't right, always disrespectin' me, always bringin' them women here and some of his old prison friends. I told him to leave and I think he mighta left town. At least I hope he did."

"Any idea where he might be or where he might have gone?"

He rubbed his face as though deep in thought.

"Knowin' him, I wouldn't be surprised if he's headed south. He hates cold weather and we got some people in Mississippi. He got a cousin up in Brookhaven. He coulda went there."

"What makes you think he's out of Detroit?"

"Man, all that time he spent up in Marquette, well, he always did hate the snow and now he really hates it. I know he's a goin' south. He done tolt me that much."

We could have continued the conversation with Mr. Dawson for hours, but I was sure he would have given us his son if he could. So we left.

Cal and I arrived back at homicide and updated the teletype. I would have the witnesses back at homicide in the morning and conduct photographic show-ups. Once he was identified it would be a simple matter of typing out the warrant request. That could wait until the morning. It had been a long and successful day and it was almost 11 p.m. when I left work and headed home.

***

The street teases you like a woman with a suggestive glance. If you chase too hard . . . you scare her. If you show faint interest . . . you bore her. It's a love-hate affair. You know you can't win . . . but you play anyhow.

The five eyewitnesses came down to homicide and each one picked out Marshall Dawson, from a photographic lineup of eight other black and white photos, as the killer of Cassie Thompson. The warrant request was a simple matter. Eye witnesses, photographic lineups, autopsy report, identifier, slam-bam-thank you ma'am. I took the warrant request to Ross Barnett who approved it, saying, "It's about time."

I noticed a wrinkled smile cross his face and nothing more was said.

I then walked the warrant request across the street to the Frank J. Murphy Hall of Justice. A bevy of assistant prosecuting attorneys were housed on the eleventh floor and as in any business a few stood out. One of the best was a young prosecutor named Tim Kennedy. Tim had earned his law degree from the University of Minnesota and gone into the public sector. He was handsome, bright, articulate, and persuasive. He had a clean look about him. He was probably earning in the neighborhood of $45,000 and often went head-to-head with defense attorneys earning twenty times more.

In my book, it was more than a fair fight. It was a wonderful thing to see Kennedy, with his Christian upbringing, not only holding his own against the street crowd but actually managing, in most cases, to beat their brains out. He was great at making the big boys look bad. His good looks and pleasant demeanor were deceiving. Underneath it all was the heart of a choirboy who sang and played with the skill of an assassin. He ranked with the best.

I took my request to him and after reading through it, he said to me, "Jack, looks like you've got a good case here. I'm recommending Murder Two. I don't see premeditation, but I see a good two."

"It sounds good to me, Tim. From everyone I've talked to, including his father, this guy is someone we need to get off the street. We've got everyone looking for him and I'm looking forward to meeting him myself. I hope you will be able to handle the trial."

I then told him about the double homicide on the freeway and the anonymous phone tip that led me to Dawson.

"I will take the case, Jack, and we will give it our best."

I knew he would.

The Honorable Rosalind Tyler Wilson

I took the file down to the signing judge, the Honorable Rosalind Tyler Wilson. She was a lovely lady. She had served on the bench for over twenty years and was an absolute legend. She was the widow of a professional athlete and her father, Mr. Donald Tyler, was a wonderful attorney who often worked for the pure joy of practicing law.

Mrs. Wilson was considered ruthless by many defense attorneys when it came time to passing sentence. This wonderful lady, who seldom raised her voice, had defendants and their attorneys shivering as they awaited justice. Most of the trials in her courtroom were decided by juries, since most defense attorneys knew that she would judge solely on the evidence and allowed little attorney showboating or smokescreens. She ran a tight ship.

On one occasion, in her court, an older man in his sixties was found guilty by the jury of second-degree murder. The crime was punishable by any number of years. The case was considered a friendly homicide where the parties knew each other. The normal sentence would usually be in the area of eight to fifteen years. This particular day, with the defendant nervously awaiting the sentence, Judge Wilson uttered, in her quiet, lady-like voice, "The Court herby sentences you to a term of no less that 35 years and no more than 60 years. The sentence is to be carried out in the State Prison of Southern Michigan located in Jackson, Michigan."

A low whoosh sound went out from the courtroom audience. The defendant said in a weakened voice, "Your Honor, I won't live that long."

The judge looked down at the man and his counselor and simply said, "We're not expecting miracles; you just do your best."

Another time, Judge Wilson was assigned to handle misdemeanor offenses. The judges at Recorder's Court used to perform that duty for fifteen-day periods and it was rotated among them. Judge Wilson smiled throughout the various proceedings and seemed to be in an unusually friendly mood that particular day. A young prostitute was brought before her. She obviously had never heard of the great lady jurist and when the testimony was completed, the defendant was found guilty of accosting and soliciting. The usual penalty for that crime was the typical slap on the wrist. Judge Wilson ordered the defendant to pay a one hundred dollar fine.

The young lady looked behind her and saw her "man" seated in the first row of the gallery. He nodded his head toward her. She then turned, looked at the judge, and said, "S---, my man's got that kind of money in his pocket."

The judges face lost all expression as she stared down the woman, her attorney and her man. The Honorable Judge Wilson took a slow breath and said, "Young lady, while your man is digging in his pocket for the money, why don't you see if he can find thirty days in the Wayne County Jail for you in there too."

Although tough on the guilty, Judge Wilson always showed concern for the victims. She quickly read over my recommended warrant request, swore me in, and signed it. She smiled at me and said, "Sergeant Loshaw, you have a great day and make sure that you're careful out there."

"Thank you, your Honor, I will."

I have always loved that lady.

The Cleveland Episode

If you stay in the casino too long you are bound to lose your money. Stay in the streets too long and you will lose your soul.

Six weeks after our warrant was issued, Detroit Homicide received some alarming news. The city of Cleveland, Ohio, had the unfortunate luck of coming into contact with Marshal Dawson. Their report read that one lone black male had entered a jewelry store and herded the owner, two clerks and three customers into the storage area. With his gun to a clerk's head, he robbed the store of several expensive pieces of jewelry. He then had the owner lock the doors and ordered all six victims into the back of the store.

In the rear storage area, the thief made all six captives kneel on the floor. After fondling the three females, he fired two .38 caliber bullets into the back of the owner's head, killing him. The smell of gunpowder floated in the air. Tears flowed down faces. The killer turned off the lights to add to the terror and kept the remaining five captives in kneeling positions. In the darkness, he chain-smoked four cigarettes while he openly discussed with himself whether they should live or die. He tried to empathize with their feelings of being powerless by saying, "I know how it feels to be treated worse than a dog." He went on to explain how he had spent a lifetime in the hole at Marquette, where he had no control. As he stood there puffing away, a smile crossed his face as he considered the wondrous feeling of having the ultimate decision over the life and death of his terrified victims.

He bragged to his captive audience that it had been surprisingly easy to kill in Detroit. He told them how much he missed the thrill of getting away with it and escaping from the long arm of the law.

He told of how he was eager to go on to bigger and better things, such as killing them.

His victims sat there, cowering, while he laughed and blew smoke into the air. Their knees were aching and hearts pounding. An hour went by and with no more cigarettes to smoke, Dawson, without explanation, calmly stood up and walked out the front door.

He had been more than careless. He never tried to cover his face. He left fingerprints throughout the store, and his gray eyes were apparent to all. He walked as if he was invincible and left behind five eyewitnesses. Ballistics later revealed the weapon used in the jewelry store murder was the same on used to kill Cassie Thompson.

> *"Power corrupts; absolute power corrupts absolutely."*
> —Henry David Thoreau

A warrant was issued in Cleveland against Dawson for Felony Murder. Ohio was one of the states that allowed for capital punishment, and Dawson would certainly rank as a candidate if convicted.

***

"The flowers appear on the earth; the time of singing has come, and the voice of the turtledove is heard in our land." Song of Solomon 2:12
What's that sound? It's the street calling me again. Ain't' no turtledove bein' heard today.

We had kept a watch on Dawson's father's place, on the Red Rooster's Lounge, and even on the blind pigs, without finding any sign of the dangerous man. I stayed in touch with the Cleveland detectives and there were no further signs of him there either. I had already contacted the authorities in Mississippi, just in case he had thoughts of visiting his kinfolk in Brookhaven and they agreed to keep an eye out for him. Finally, four months after the Cleveland murder he struck again. He found himself in Tallahassee, Florida, where he decided that two little prostitutes had served their purpose and killed them. His father had been right about him heading south.

The two girls in Florida had extensive records for accosting and soliciting. Dawson had run into them in an after-hours establishment, invited them to his place, and, after flashing lots of money, offered to party with them. The party was not much fun for them. After he had enjoyed himself for a couple of hours, he decided that playtime was over and produced a gun. Apparently sex had not satisfied his desires, so he slapped them around for a while. One of the girls managed to run out the side door, but Dawson chased after her and dragged her by the hair back to the room. He tied the girls up, placed a pillow over their heads, and fired three shots into their faces. The bullets matched the Cleveland case. The guy had been carrying around a murder weapon for over four months! I was convinced that he really did think he was invincible. I sent his photos to Tallahassee. His fingerprints were all over the place, again, and witnesses at the after-hours joint and the motel easily identified his mug shots.

I was beginning to really dislike this man.

***

They ought to call the streets after that woman who messed up Samson. She enticed him, loved him, put him to sleep, and then turned him over to the Man. What was her name?

124

Eighteen months after Cassie Thompson's murder, Dawson was arrested in Seattle, Washington. The report stated that he had beaten his girlfriend-prostitute up pretty well. Supposedly, he was pimping, and she was his prime moneymaker. Seattle cops arrived at the scene and arrested Dawson without incident. He was taken to the local precinct, where one of the arresting officers confiscated a heavy gold chain from his neck. It was similar to the chain that Mr. T, of the *Rocky* movies, had made popular. Mr. Dawson was unable to provide any means of economic existence so his expensive, though cheap looking, chain was taken away. The arresting officer put the gold rope on an evidence tag and figured to check with the B&E Squad to see if it was a stolen item.

A couple of hours after his arrest, the victim showed up demanding that her man be set free. She said that her injuries were self-inflicted and told of her great love for dear Marsh. Then the unimaginable happened. Marshall Dawson was released. For some unexplained reason, his prints were never sent to the Federal authorities. After he had been discharged the mistake was discovered. His prints were quickly sent out and just as rapidly the tilt light went on. He was wanted in three different states and the police officers went on red-alert trying to locate and recapture Dawson. Heads were going to roll.

Hubris is a great word that describes excessive pride and Dawson could have posed for the centerfold for *Hubris Monthly*. This man, so full of pride, had no idea that half of the Seattle Police Department was out looking for him. At just past 9:30 p.m., he came strolling back into the precinct demanding to have his gold necklace returned to him. He was quickly rearrested and held for murder in Detroit, Cleveland and Tallahassee.

A huge sigh of relief came from the desk staff at the precinct.

A couple of Detroit officers, assigned to the Extradition Unit, flew out to Seattle and brought Dawson back to Motown.

The Detectives from Cleveland

Once Dawson was safely in our custody, I notified the Cleveland Police Department of his arrest. I was told they were sending a team to Detroit to interview the dangerous one. The team consisted of two dedicated detectives named Milosic and Gancos. While they were at the airport an anonymous call came through 911 reporting that there was a contract out on them. Supposedly, a sum of $50,000 was payable upon their deaths. This was more than troublesome to the two men and to us. Very few people had any idea who was assigned to the Dawson case, and even less had the wherewithal to issue that size of a contract. Who did Dawson know? Why would anyone even think about killing cops for a loser like him? Who was supplying the money? This kind of stuff didn't happen in real life. In the few contract cases that I had run into, the amounts of money never approached fifty thousand dollars. Ohio had the death penalty, of course, so the stakes were definitely higher.

The two detectives were not at all pleased to hear of the price on their heads. It was flattering that so much money was being talked about, but this was a little more than they had bargained for. When they arrived at my office they played it off as best as they could, but I could tell it made them edgy. We offered them a couple of bulletproof vests which were accepted with appreciation.

I shared my case with them and gave as much insight into Dawson as I could. My interview with Marshall had lasted less than two minutes. In this time he made it clear he would never talk to me and assured me that he had the ability to make sure that I would die of something less than natural causes. I was starting to wonder if a contract had been put out on me. It was a matter of principle, and being a bit competitive by nature, I was hoping it was for a lot more than the Cleveland guys. The two detectives had even less success than I had with Dawson, and the interview never went beyond him cursing and spewing saliva at them. They went back to Cleveland hoping Dawson would never get out of the Michigan Prison System.

My boss, Ross Barnett, encouraged me to be careful. His exact words were: "Don't go getting yourself killed. One of these days, if everything breaks right, you've got a chance to be a decent detective and I don't want to start breaking in someone to replace you just yet."

He had a smirkey smile that let me know this was as close to a compliment as I would ever get from him. I gave him a returned smirk and said, "I've got this great big six-shot Colt Cobra here to protect me, so don't go worrying, boss."

"Yeah, right. I've seen your shooting scores at the range. You better get a nine millimeter, maybe the noise from it will scare 'em to death."

I did start watching my rear end, though. I figured that the whole thing was like something right out of Hollywood but, nevertheless, I started being a little more careful. I took different routes home each night. I kept a close eye on my rearview mirror and I drove different cars as often as I could. One night, while cruising down Gratiot on the way home, I noticed three handsome looking fellows in a dark Ford keeping an eye on me. I busted a red light to see if they were serious, but they stayed back. After a few minutes I noticed them getting a little closer, so I made a quick right onto a side street, jumping out of my car, I and pulled my six-shooter out and held it down by my belt. The Ford came wheeling around the corner, saw me with the gun, and went racing by. I gave the plate out and as expected, it was stolen. I never saw the guys or that car again, and I really don't know if they were after me or not. Anyhow, I'm still alive today, so . . .

I told Inspector Barnett what had happened and he became furious.

"This Dawson thinks he's some kind of bad a--, huh? Maybe I'll go up there and have a face to face with him."

His face had taken on that reddish gray color and I knew he was hot. I don't know if that meeting ever took place but I would have paid anything to have been a witness to it. In many ways, I was proud to have him worrying about me.

Jimmy

J. Wayne Clepper was a defense attorney who earned in excess of a quarter million dollars a year. Most human beings believed that he didn't have a pulse and in his case it was not a requirement. His main client was a group called Young Boys Incorporated. YBI was a vicious group of street gangsters who specialized in the dope street traffic trade—they only used boys age eleven to fourteen as deliverers and lookouts for the heroin packets they pushed. Many of these boys would make five to six hundred dollars a week, which was enough to purchase the best Nikes the malls had to offer. The gang was actually quite sophisticated, even to the point of having the initials YBI stamped on their heroin packets.

The leaders of the gang were two well-known street thugs named Ronald "Rolex" Jones and Raylen "The People's Choice" Peeples. The names sounded like they should have belonged to prizefighters on the Kronk boxing team. In just over four years, this gang was responsible for thirty-six murders, countless rapes, maimings, and general mayhem. J. Wayne Clepper was their attorney. He was very vocal about letting law enforcement officers know that for the sum of $10,000 per month he would respond to any police precinct whenever a member of the gang was detained. He was on call and "freely" offered his legal advice to Jones and Peeples.

For all his wealth, Mr. Clepper always looked grubby and unkempt. He wore expensive suits that somehow appeared ill-fitting and cheap. His hair was bushy and in need of combing. His tie was never tight and against his dusty complexion even his white shirt appeared dingy. He was short in stature, at five foot six inches, weighed in excess of 200 pounds and had very little body tone. Clepper was certainly a prospect for a class with the Vic Tanney fitness club and a likely candidate for a heart attack. Of course that would have been considered wishful thinking on the part of many police officers.

J. Wayne's face was covered with little dark indentations caused by ingrown whiskers, which added to his unkempt appearance. His chin was adorned with a goatee he had hoped would look menacing. However, due to irregular hair growth, it looked splotchy and added to his slovenly looks. He had some gold work done on his teeth. If his dental work was done to enhance his

128

looks, then he had wasted his money. If his efforts were to impress his fellow lawyers and clients, then they were rousingly successful. However, his efforts were dismal failures if they were done to impress any warm-blooded creatures. As you can probably tell by now, Mr. Clepper did not rate highly on my list of most likeable people.

He was like so many other defense attorneys, to whome right and wrong were not considerations. Winning was all that counted. Being heartless and uncaring, plus having a perverted lust for money were essential qualities for success and J. Wayne Clepper had PhDs in all three. In reality, he was barely adequate as a barrister. He was blustery for sure—lots of show and very little go. If I was on trial, there were scores of lawyers that I would have chosen before him. But he fit the style of YBI with his arrogance and total disregard for authority.

One day, while leaving court, I hopped on an already crowded elevator. Mr. Clepper was there with his entourage. If I had noticed him on the elevator before the door closed, I would have walked the nine flights to the main floor.

In an effort to impress his head-nodders, he asked me, "Well, how's the killing business, detective?"

"It's something that happens . . . Mr. Clepper. I'm sure that brings a way for you to earn a living."

"Don't worry about me making a living. I've been living in the high-rent district for a long time and I plan on stayin' there."

I knew Clepper was used to hearing questions whispered to him so I said quietly, "By the way, what does the *J* stand for in your name?

He responded in a voice louder than necessary, "It stands for James, but I never use it 'cause I don't want you white folks calling me Jim."

There were some approving chuckles from his gang. That same gang that had somehow learned to bow from the knees whenever he came around.

The doors opened to the main floor and as I was stepping out I turned to the great counselor and said, "See you around, Jimmy."

I heard a deep and unintelligible guttural noise coming from the esteemed lawyer.

The Trial

It has been said the wheels of justice move slowly. Twenty three months had passed and finally the trial was about to begin. The date was July 17, 1982. Cassie Thompson would have been twenty-four years old and had missed a Christmas and two of her birthdays.

I walked over to the courthouse, took the elevator up to the seventh floor, and entered Judge Leonard Stoner's courtroom. Someone had warned the judge that this particular defendant came with a bad reputation. The judge had heeded the advice and there were five very burly Wayne County Sheriff Deputies in attendance. Security was not going to be a problem; Judge Stoner was not one to be considered foolhardy.

I took my seat at the prosecutor's table, where the assistant prosecuting attorney, Tim Kennedy, was already seated. He was busy studying the case file when he looked up and said, "How you doing, Jack?"

"I'm okay, how 'bout you?"

"I'm ready. You ready?"

"You bet. All the witnesses have been served subpoenas and there shouldn't be any problem with them being here to testify. I've talked to each one and they are anxious to get this over."

I was thinking about how important this case was to me. My daughter, Kathy, was fourteen at the time and I couldn't help but think of her and Cassie and their many similarities. Both were so pretty, so smart, one streetwise and the other a cop's kid who was gathering lots of street smarts. One was so alive, and the other so . . .

In my career, I had probably testified dozens of times in murder cases. I was pretty good at it and pretty convincing, most times. Juries seemed to like me. I tried to come across as confident, but not as a know-it-all. One defense attorney told the jury at the closing argument that they shouldn't be swayed by me because, "He comes across as a Madison Avenue–style detective, with his smooth words and engaging smile, but all he wants to do is put someone in jail just so he can close his case!"

Now that was hypocrisy if I'd ever heard it!

Another time, an attorney told the jury, "In front of you, ladies and gentlemen, he comes across as a velvet glove, but in reality when he's dealing with less refined people (like his client, of course) he comes across like the iron fist. Don't be fooled by him!"

In both of those cases the jurors didn't buy what the attorneys were selling and brought back guilty verdicts. My point is this—every time I took a case to trial, I felt that I was on trial. My work was put under a microscope and examined by the prying eyes of the defense. Cassie Thompson's case had become very close to me, and I was nervous. I was also wired, keyed, excited, and anxious. I had asked God, as I had on many other times, for His favor and that the truth would come to light.

At precisely 9 a.m., Judge Stoner took the bench. Mr. J. Wayne Clepper, Esquire, had already entered the courtroom carrying a black-leather Guitton briefcase full of legal papers and was seated at the defense table. At that moment, two deputies brought Mr. Dawson from the holding area, unshackled him, and escorted him to Clepper's table. There, they embraced each other and said something in Arabic, just loud enough for all to know that they were members of some exclusive club. Mr. Dawson was clad in a very nice, dark-blue suit, white shirt, maroon-colored tie, and high glossed black shoes. He looked like he had just left a board meeting of the Detroit Bank and Trust. They sat down and Mr. Clepper rummaged through his briefcase. He fished out a King James Bible, a pair of wire-rimmed glasses, and handed them to Marshall Dawson. With all the props in place, the trial was about to begin.

Mr. Clepper was known as one expensive attorney. Tim Kennedy leaned over and said, "Where is the money coming from to pay Clepper?"

"I don't know, but someone is fronting this whole scene," I answered.

A panel of sixty prospective jurors was brought into the courtroom. The judge informed them of the nature of the case and expressed his gratitude for their appearance. That having been said, the judge then explained the legal process called *voir dire* in which the attorneys question the jurors hoping to find a fair and impartial group. In reality, they hoped to find a group who would support their side and either convict or acquit depending on what side of the law they were on. The process of selecting a jury was often tedious and time consuming, as would likely be the case this time. At 12:30 p.m., only six jurors had been selected and court was dismissed for lunch. After the break, the pace quickened and the remaining eight jurors were chosen. Lunch had apparently hastened the process. The jury consisted of ten women and four men. At the close of the trial, two members would randomly be eliminated and the twelve remaining ones would decide the case. I was pleased, thinking that the women would be sympathetic to Cassie. Mr. Clepper, always the charmer, looked pleased too, thinking that he would be able to draw on their maternal instincts so they would look favorably upon his poor, misunderstood client.

All during the *voir dire,* Marshall Dawson was either intently studying the Bible, or looking as affable and pleasant as possible. All the while, I was silently praying that the truth would come out and that every deception would be exposed.

I looked over at the defense table and a very strange, almost eerie thing happened. I could see a vapor like substance rising from the table. I rubbed my eyes, thinking that I had strained them, but the vapor remained for another moment and then vanished. I realized that I was witnessing evil personified in the presence of Clepper and Dawson. They seemed to me to be soul-mates of the lowest order.

The trial proceeded as expected with the prosecutor, Kennedy, presenting the medical examiner, the identifier, and the five key witnesses. Dawson had been easily identified by his photographs, his live show-ups, and now in court. Of course, he looked rather dapper with his new threads, reading glasses, and his ever-present Holy Bible. He hardly looked threatening at all. As was usually the case, the first part of the trial was heavily weighted in the prosecution's favor. Mr. Clepper was smart enough not to make anyone look too bad, at this point.

It was clear to us that the only argument the defense could make was that of self-defense. And now the only other question we had was, "will Dawson take the stand?"

On the third day, Spencer Thompson, Cassie's father, collapsed in the hall and was rushed to Detroit General Hospital. He had suffered a heart attack but was expected to survive. It seemed like the streets were claiming another victim.

On the fourth day, the People rested their case and Clepper stated that he would present three character witnesses on behalf of his client. The first one was an elderly man who had known Dawson for the last six months. That, of course, was during the time that Dawson was being held in the Wayne County Jail. The gentleman was a lay preacher who saw only the good in people. His vision had to be better than 20/20 to see any good in Dawson, as far as I was concerned. The next witness was a man who had served time with Dawson in Marquette. He, too, had only good things to say about the defendant. Mr. Kennedy brought out the facts, from the same witness, that Dawson was considered one of the cruelest convicts in the penitentiary and it became obvious that Clepper regretted putting him on the stand. The third witness bolted from the courthouse during the testimony of Dawson's fellow inmate and never did testify. Finally, the defense called its star witness, Marshall Dawson.

***

As they say out there in the streets, "what goes around comes around." There is always someone out their sellin' wolf tickets and sho' 'nuff there is always someone out there lookin' to buy one.

133

Dawson's Testimony

Marshall Dawson walked to the witness stand, looked at the court clerk, and raised his right hand. He affirmed to tell the truth, the whole truth, and nothing but the truth. He sat down, unbuttoned his suit jacket, crossed one leg over the other, smiled at the jury, and turned to face Mr. Clepper.

His attorney, in a delicate way, began the journey of Marshall's life. He was able to elicit from Dawson his unfortunate upbringing, his lack of proper education, his experimentation with drugs, and in general his exposure to the street life. Indeed, life had dealt him a bad hand that brought him to his present state of gratuitous violence.

As a teenager, he had learned the art of street thuggery. Early in life that homosexuals were easy targets. He practiced the art of "fairy hawkin," as he called it. Before his esteemed counselor could get him to quiet down, Dawson explained that all that was required of him was to pretend interest in a "date" and at the appropriate time, beat the homosexual senseless while robbing him of all his valuables. He let the jury know that because there were very few opportunities for normal employment, he had become very skilled at robbing people. Plus it was easier.

Mr. Clepper's face was controlled by a slight grimace, as Dawson rattled on about his exploits. On two occasions the lawyer attempted to quiet Dawson. Unable to do so, he flashed a toothy smile at the jury as if to say, "He said it, not me."

Through the clever questioning of his attorney, Dawson continued his story.

By the time he reached fifteen he graduated to armed robbery. During an eighteen-month period, he was brought before the juvenile authorities four times for robbery incidents. He could not recall the number of times he was kept at the Juvenile Home, but admitted that he had been there a "few" times.

Dawson then told of the arrest that took him to Jacktown and eventually Marquette State Prison. He went into detail about the unfair treatment he received while incarcerated. Guards were always bringing up false charges accusing him and creating reasons to have him isolated. It was probably because of his gray eyes, or the fact that he wasn't a "yes" man. He told of the horrors of being kept in solitary confinement for a period of years. The only entertainment he had was body building. He worked on doing two hundred pushups at a time, plus the hundreds of chin-ups and . . . Clepper tried to stop his client's bragging, but it was too late. Dawson continued, "I could even do seventy-five pushups with one of my fellows laying on my back, and I did a lot of shadow boxing just to stay in rhythm." With this last statement Clepper was finally able to break in with a question about the night the victim was tragically killed.

Mr. Kennedy objected and before the Court could rule . . .

"Her name is Cassie Thompson! She was not just a victim, she had a name."

Mr. Clepper ignored the statement and asked, "What was your relationship with the deceased?"

Mr. Kennedy stood up and said, "Her name was Cassie Thompson!"

It should have been clear how Clepper, with his usual lack of tact, had transformed her from a person to an item.

The judge intervened and Clepper asked it again, "The victim, Miss Thompson, what was your relationship with her?"

"I'd been knowin' her for 'bout a mont', before her death . . . we was gettin' it on pretty good."

Mr. Clepper smiled at Dawson and asked him to explain, "What do you mean by, getting it on?"

"I mean, she was likin' me."

Clepper seemed a little surprise as he raised his eyebrows. "Had you been dating her?"

"Well, not like goin' out and stuff, but we had some drinks together, and I could tell, you know, that she was diggin' me. Anybody coulda seen that."

"Did you ever have any words with her?"

"No, not really. 'Cept one night I had bought her some drinks and stuff, and axed her to come over to my place and she tolt me that I was bold or somethin'. I tolt her that I didn't appreciate her disrespectin' me and stuff, but I never hit her or nothin'."

"On the night of her death, can you tell the court what happened?"

"Yes. We was suppose to have this date, and when I got there she was up there dancin' with this dude. I reached over and tapped her on the shoulder."

"Are you saying that you did not squeeze her buttocks?"

"I sure didn't, and anyone that says I did is a liar. All I did was tap her on her shoulder."

"What happened then?"

"She got this attitude, you see, and jumped in my face and slapped me."

"What happened then?"

"I waited for the dance to end and I went to her and axed her why she slapped me. The next thing I know she was goin' for a bottle and I did what I had to do."

With that, Marshall wiped his mouth with the back of his hand. He had a pained expression on his face as if remembering that night had brought deep sorrow to him. I kept waiting for tears to well up in those scary gray eyes.

"What was it, Mr. Dawson, that you had to do?"

This next part, it appeared, had been committed to memory.

"Well, you know, most of my life, I've been treated like an animal."

With each utterance his voice was changing. The pitch intensified. There was a horrible squealing quality to it. It was something I had never heard coming from a human being before. The closest sound that I can compare it to is that of a fan belt slipping. It was eerie.

"And all I could think of was survival. I was in fear of my life."

I looked at the faces of the jury panel to see their reactions. They, too, appeared aggravated by his squealing voice. The words that came out of his mouth did not evoke sympathy, but, rather, disgust.

"Mr. Dawson, are you saying that a 112 pound woman put you in fear of your life?"

"When she got holt of that bottle it sure did. All my life I have had to protect myself. It was eat or be eaten, ya know? It's been that way my whole life. When I saw what she was tryin' to do, I had to protect myself. I had a gun because I knew the place was a rough joint and without even thinking I shot her. I'm real sorry that she died, but what was I to do, just let her do what she wanted to do?"

"Your witness, Mr. Prosecutor."

Tim Kennedy lived for moments like this and was eager for a go at Mr. Dawson. He sat for a long moment and finally whispered to me, "Jack, I think he's buried himself. I'm almost afraid to go after him though. I think Clepper did most of my work for me. I don't want to bury him so deep that the jury starts feeling sorry for him. What do you think?"

"Clepper made him out to act like he was a wounded animal. Show him for what he is."

With that Mr. Kennedy stepped to the box. "How many people have you killed?"

"Objection!"

"Sustained."

"Did you grab Miss Thompson by the buttocks?"

"No."

"We've produced five witnesses who have testified that you did grab her by the buttocks."

"They lied. I had people lyin' on me my whole life."

"When she finished dancing, did you grab her breasts?"

"No."

"So the five witnesses who have testified that you did are telling lies?"

"Yeah, they probably been tolt what to say and they was all friends of that girl."

"After you put the gun to within an inch or two of her face, and fired into her, did you do anything to help her?"

"Would you help someone who had just tried to hurt you?"

"Answer the question, please."

"No, I was scared and I just ran outta there."

"What did you do with the gun?"

"I threw it in some dumpster."

Along with just about everyone else in the courtroom, I was ready to puke.

"Are you sure about that?"

"Um, I dunno. I think I might have kept it for a while."

"Well, just how long did you keep it? Did you take it to Cleveland?"

Clepper jumped to his feet and screamed, "Objection! What's Cleveland got to do with it?"

To which Mr. Kennedy replied, "You need to ask your client."

Kennedy only asked a few more questions. It was clear that Dawson's self-defense argument was in serious trouble.

Mr. Clepper tried to rehabilitate his client with the re-direct examination without success. The attorneys rested their cases.

The closing arguments were brief. Clepper, having read the juror's faces, realized that his self-defense strategy had failed. He now called upon them to exercise the noblest of human qualities—mercy. Mr. Kennedy only asked them to render a fair verdict.

Of course, with the law being the law, the jury panel was never told of all the other murder charges that Dawson was facing.

The jurors were sent to deliberate. After a little over two hours later they sent word back that they had reached a unanimous verdict.

Guilty as charged.

Dawson then dropped all pretenses. His glasses came off. He shoved his Bible across the table and onto the floor. He began screaming, again in that irritating high frequency squeal, and spit out profanities by the scores. Four of the court deputies surrounded the defense table. His gray eyes had that icy stare to them and as he glared at me, he vowed, "Loshaw, you'll be dead in a month, you -------!"

I tried my best to hold his glare and said, "Yeah, well I'm not some twenty-two year old girl." The courtroom was a powder keg by now. The deputies quickly took custody of Dawson, and the frightened jurors were ushered out of the courtroom into the hall.

I congratulated the prosecutor on doing his usual excellent job, and walked out into the hall. The jurors were all talking at once, like high school kids, enjoying the freedom of escaping the court confines and the presence of the evil happenings here. Several came up to me and wished me well. I promised them that I would do my best to outlive Mr. Dawson and his esteemed attorney. I then told them that there were at least three other murder charges facing Dawson. I saw some of them take deep breaths, knowing that they had not only fulfilled their civic duties but would now also sleep better at night. To my surprise, I received hugs from several of them.

When I left the courthouse I walked the one block over to the Detroit Receiving Hospital where I learned that Mr. Thompson was recovering. I told him of the courtroom events and decisions. A smile of deep satisfaction spread over his face. He said words that I'll never forget. "Sergeant, he took my little girl. I hurt so bad. Probably always will. I know I should hate him, but I don't. Don't get me wrong, I don't like him, but I don't hate him. Thanks for getting him. From the bottom of my heart, thanks. Thank you, sir."

I shook his hand and thanked him for his testimony and his kind words. His appreciation meant more to me than anyone would ever know.

The sentencing date was set for July 31, 1982.

Three days prior to sentencing I had a talk with my boss, Barnett, and told him I wanted to go to the jail and talk with Dawson. I hoped that he might talk about his other murders. Barnett told me it was a waste of time but wished me luck.

Dawson was quartered in the special security section of the Wayne County Jail. I had a glimmering hope that he might want to brag about his other killings. He saw me coming, and a torrent of expletives came gushing out of his mouth. He, again, promised to have me and mine murdered in the most horrendous way. Finally, he stopped. I told him of my purpose.

He said, "You must think that I am the dumbest n----- on the earth. I wouldn't tell you, of all people, anything. You ain't nothin' but a peckerwood."

Now, I've been called lots of things, but that was a first. I walked down the corridor, smiling to myself, wondering about being named a peckerwood.

When I arrived back at Homicide, I bumped into one of the older black officers, named A. C. Williams. He was a dedicated man who had worked in the unit four years past his retirement. I told him about Dawson and our conversation. A. C. told me, "That man doesn't sound like he likes you none. You see, in the South, one of the worst things you can call a white man is peckerwood. After the Civil War, the northerners who came down south and swindled the poor white folks out of their possessions and lands were called 'carpetbaggers.' The southerners who did the same were called peckerwoods. So, brother, that man done insulted you the most possible way."

I thanked A.C., closed up for the day and went home. And as usual my wife, Pat, asked me as she usually did, "Did you put any bad guys in jail today?"

And my typical answer: "Yep, just one today."

The sentence given by Judge Leonard Stoner to Marshall Dawson was 75 to 125 years for the murder charge, and two years for using a firearm in the commission of a felony. With any luck, Marshall could get out when he reached 108. Of course, he would still have to answer to the pending cases in other states.

As a homicide detective I met some evil people, but I had never met anyone like Dawson. It seemed to me that he enjoyed inflicting pain, the taking of lives and being wicked for the sake of being wicked.

The Law of the Jungle
By Rudyard Kipling

Now this is the Law of the Jungle,
As old and as true as the sky,
And the wolf that shall keep it may prosper,
But the wolf that shall break it must die.

And the creeper that girdles the tree-trunk,
The Law runneth forward and back,
For the strength of the pack is the wolf,
And the strength of the wolf is the pack.

Chapter Ten: Why Would Anyone Care?

It was February 18, 1982, when a phone call came into the Homicide Desk. A downtown unit reported that a homeless person had found a dead body in a mound of melting snow. The body was in such a state of decomposition that it was impossible to tell if the death was natural. The location was south of Jefferson Avenue, less than one quarter of a mile from the Detroit River. I responded to the scene along with Evidence Technician Drew Neal.

The city of Detroit had undergone an unseasonably warm February day and the sun was beginning to penetrate the ice and snow that had covered the city for weeks. The vagrant had been prowling the alleys looking for anything of value when he came across a thin right arm sticking out through the snow. He walked around hoping to find a police officer or anyone else he could tell of his finding. It was also the first time in his life that he had actually sought out a police officer; usually they found him. He felt fortunate to spot two police officers in a coffee shop on Jefferson Avenue and was able to convince them of what he had discovered. The officers considered putting him in the backseat of their car for directions, but after noticing his foul odor they decided it best to have him lead them by foot to the scene. The officers dug through enough of the snow to know that the victim appeared to be a black female in an advanced state of decay. The officers made the call to Homicide.

The alley was in a desolate area of abandoned warehouses. Most of the structures had been earmarked for demolition. The current mayor had spent months twisting arms of business and civic leaders in hopes of having a new ballpark built on that very site. There was little doubt that he had visions of the park being named in his honor.

I drove into the alley and directed the evidence technician to prepare a sketch and take photographs. There were no doors to be knocked on and the only witness was the homeless man. The real work would have to be performed by the doctors at the Wayne County Morgue. I, along with the uniformed men, stood waiting for the morgue truck to arrive. My feet were freezing, so I quickly took a statement from the vagrant, sent him on his way, and went to the warmth of my car. The wagon arrived and two attendants stepped out. The senior of the two was Jim Baty, "Pretty day, Sarge, but still kinda cold."

"No kidding, Jim. It's gonna take some work to get this woman out of the ice. Did you bring a blow torch?"

"No problem. We always carry a little heat gun for things like this."

With that they pawed away at the snow, using the heat gun to free her from the larger blocks of ice. It was soon clear that she was nude. I had the evidence tech take a few pictures and then she was zipped up in a leather bag, loaded onto a stretcher, and taken to the morgue.

The body was labeled as Jane Doe #145. It took some time for her body to thaw enough so that the doctors could perform an autopsy. She was a black female, from twenty to fifty years of age, approximately 5'2", with short black hair, and extremely thin despite the fact that her body was bloated by decomposition. There was no way to tell from looking at her whether she had suffered any wounds. After her body had thawed the smell inside the autopsy room was much more pronounced than it had been at the scene. It always amazed me that the morgue doctors could perform their duties with the horrible stench of decomposition penetrating their clothes and filling their noses.

I called for an officer from the identification section to come to the morgue. He put a healthy dose of Vicks Vapor Rub in his nose and did what he could to take her fingerprints. He called me thirty minutes later to tell me he had matched them to a Lorraine Davis. Lorraine Davis was thirty-two years old with a long record of prostitution and drug use. I learned from going through her file that she had no known relatives, no recorded addresses, and the only name that was ever mentioned was that of a friend, Willie Harvey. It crossed my mind that he was probably her pimp.

I went through Harvey's record in our identification section and came up with a mug shot. My partner Cal Noles and I drove out to one of his most recent addresses and showed his photo around. We visited a few "ladies of the night" walking Woodward Avenue and dropped his name at a few places.

After knocking on a few doors of his previous haunts, we went back to 1300 Beaubien. It didn't take long before the phones started ringing about Harvey. It seemed that there were plenty of street folks who would have been pleased to have him off the streets. Most of the callers were women.

***

Lorraine Davis was a prostitute . . . just a street prostitute . . . often considered the lowest of the street people. Now she was a dead prostitute. It didn't matter. Why would anyone care? In death she existed as Jane Doe #145 and because her body had decomposed so badly, it took some time before we learned her real identity. Lorraine Davis. She had no middle name . . . as if to say a single name was enough for her. She had no next of kin. And I thought to myself, "what an amazing statement—no next of kin. Heck, everyone had a next of kin!" But not Jane Doe #145.

The cause of death was determined, after much testing, to have been from manual strangulation. Her killer would have looked into her eyes, saw the terror in her face, and then squeezed the life from her. So what . . . she was just a street prostitute.

***

After the first phone calls, it became easy to locate Willie Harvey. He had been known to hang around Red Benson's pool hall on Linwood and Philadelphia. He wasn't hard to spot. He fit his description well: black male, 6'2", 240 pounds, dark complexion, full goatee, and bushy Afro-style hair with a large bald spot at the top. Word had spread that we were looking for him and he acted like he was expecting us when Cal and I walked into the pool hall.

He was shooting snooker with another man who quickly put his stick away and strolled out the rear door. There was no need to identify ourselves as police officers. It had been years since white folks had entered that establishment; plus we looked a lot more like cops than we did investment bankers. I told him that we needed to talk and we would have to do our talking downtown. He mumbled a few words in protest and after a few seconds placed his stick on the rack and came out to the car. Cal joined him in the back seat and I drove to Homicide.

Willie Harvey had been in the presence of police officers many times. However, this was his first exposure to the Homicide Unit. I poured him a cup of coffee, had him seated at my desk, and after some preliminaries we began a serious conversation regarding the murder of Lorraine Davis. He tried to act very nonchalant . . . as if he was used to dealing with the big time events, like murder. He was, after all, the "man" out on the street. He was the one person many of the street people feared, especially women. I sat at my desk with the typewriter in front of me and put a couple of blank papers into the machine. He was seated at the left corner of my desk, trying to stifle a yawn or two. I was getting aggravated with his "I just don't give a damn" attitude.

He began to brag that years ago he had watched over a couple of girls working for him. He enjoyed pimping but was too generous to be really good at it.

"I let them keep some of their money. My problem was, I was just too nice, you know what I mean?" While he was talking he kept checking his manicured fingernails.

"Oh, I can see that you're the kind of guy that would worry about his women. You come across as a decent man," I replied.

He smiled and began to think that he and I were a lot alike.

He actually fancied himself as being a pleasant sort of man who was gentle with his girls. Harvey told of how it pained him to have to slap them around. It bothered his conscience to take the money, but if he didn't then someone else surely would. He seemed to have the feeling that I understood his dilemma while all the time I was becoming more disgusted with each sentence. With every breath he cursed and showed no respect for Lorraine or the hopeless life she had led. I was quickly tiring of hearing about his kindness and generosity as I steered the conversation to back Lorraine.

Throughout the investigation I was particularly saddened by the fact that

Lorraine Davis had lived a life without any apparent purpose. Her life had meant little or nothing to anyone, and that was disturbing to me. It was disgusting that there was no one who cared one bit whether she lived or died. She was like a "no deposit, no return" bottle that would only clutter the landscape. Somehow her murder had become a very personal matter to me.

I seldom talked to my wife about an active case, but I did mention that Lorraine Davis had led a life in which nobody cared about her. My wife comforted me by saying, "She did matter. Her death has caused you to care, and that means something."

Her words helped.

During the interrogation of Mr. Harvey, I'm sure he had no idea that he was touching a raw nerve. What happened next was probably a greater surprise to me and the three other detectives in the room than it was to Harvey.

"Willie, can you tell me anything about Lorraine that might give me some insight as to who might have killed her?"

"All I can tell you, man, is that for an ugly little broad, she was one great lay."

THWACK!

I am not sure as to the moment in time when premeditation is determined. Does it take much planning? Can it be decided in a millisecond? Does it bypass the brain and cause a person to just react?

I had done something that was totally out of character.

The moment he finished the word "lay" I threw out my left arm and with the back of my hand slapped him across his face. The suddenness and force of the blow surprised and jarred him and I saw him for what I suspected he was, a coward. His face had turned ashen as he threw his hands up to cover his face. He cowered, expecting more blows, as I bolted out of my seat and said, "Now, let's try this again. Tell me about Lorraine Davis! And another thing, I am sick and tired of your swearing, so I recommend that you speak English, do you understand?"

147

He straightened up and said, "What do you want to know, sir?"

I thought to myself, "Sir? He called me sir! What a wimp! Is force the only thing that he respects?"

The remainder of our conversation took just over two hours. Somehow he managed to give me a fairly intelligent statement and only swore on two occasions . . . and immediately apologized each time. I felt badly that he really didn't add anything significant to the case. When I finished talking to him, I called for a scout car to convey him back to the pool hall where I was sure he would tell them of the terrible brutality he had suffered.

When the uniformed crew arrived, I walked up to Harvey and, while tapping my right index finger below his collarbone, said, "I'm going to be in your neighborhood on a regular basis and I want to make sure we maintain our ongoing friendship."

He was at a loss for words as he walked away. I was pretty sure that he didn't want me as a friend.

After he was gone, Patrick Brown, one of the detectives in the squad, came up to me and threw his arm around my shoulder. He said, "Jack, when you slapped him, that was one of the coolest things I've ever seen. I almost fell over. I couldn't believe you would ever do something like that. Man, you even scared me some. Then I looked at your partner, Noles, and I don't think he knew whether to run, jump, or yell. You caught us all by surprise."

"Well, I'm not feeling too good about myself right now, Pat. I wish I hadn't done it, but I can't undo it now. I couldn't bring myself to apologize to him, but it won't happen again."

"It would be okay with me if it happened all the time. I think you did the right thing. I love you, man!"

"Thanks." These were the guys who had seen me change. The same guys who had asked me the questions about my relationship with God and about the changes that had occurred in my life. I hoped I hadn't blown everything.

What an idiot I had been to damage my testimony just because one jerk got the best of me. I thought of the time in the Bible when David had put on the armor of Saul to go face Goliath. The armor didn't fit. And that day I had done something that didn't fit . . . and I was sick to my heart.

***

I worked on the case for two weeks and never solved it. I never came close to solving it. We knew there was a serial killer out terrorizing and killing prostitutes. We knew he had murdered more than twelve women. Women who had been strangled manually or through ligature, and the vast majority were prostitutes. The killer became known as "Bigfoot." The street girls, who had reported a huge black man that had severely beaten several of the girls and they had dubbed him so. Many "Johns" were arrested and interrogated and finally a suspect named Pantross was arrested. He was a basketball player on scholarship in Iowa. During spring break he was caught in Detroit beating a prostitute. A search warrant of his Highland Park home produced a collection of over two hundred pair of female underwear he kept as reminder trophies. After several hours of interrogation he was charged with three counts of first degree murder.

All of us at Homicide were convinced he was the murderer.

Twenty-three months after the discovery of Lorrain Davis's body, a scout car crew in the Fourth Precinct came across some action in a car in a "lovers lane" area near the Rouge River Bridge. As it turned out, they interrupted a brutal sexual attack of a prostitute by a man named Randolph Williams. He was arrested and, in time, confessed and convinced all that he was indeed the "Bigfoot" who had killed the women. He openly bragged and seemed to enjoy the power he exercised as he strangled the women. He had no record and there had been no reason for anyone to suspect him of evil. He was a model citizen who had stored wickedness in his heart and took it out on those trusting souls of the night.

After his trial, Williams was convicted and sentenced to life without parole. The attorney for Pantross sued the city, won big money, and the collector of panties walked as a free man.

Chapter Eleven: Is There Not A Cause?

As David looked over Goliath and the Philistine army he said, "Is there not a cause?"
I Samuel 17:29

It was a nice June day in 1982 and I had just finished two days off when, at 5:30 a.m., I was awakened by the telephone and the gentle loving voice of my squad lieutenant, Reg Hart.

Reg had been one of the first black detectives brought into the Homicide Unit and had proven himself through fourteen years in the unit. He was sure of himself and helped create that assurance in the men he supervised. He had now reached the age of fifty, was still physically fit, and was able to work late into the night without wavering. Many detectives envied him because he was cited often in the newspapers and as I often said to him, "There isn't a microphone that you have ever ignored."

"Heck, that ain't nothin' Jack. You should see me when there's a TV camera," he said with his crooked smile.

Reg always had something to say...and said it. He was confident and acted like it. He was disliked by many because he was thought to be a publicity hound, but he didn't care what most people thought. He only cared about those who knew him and I was one of those.

"Good morning, Jackie. Did you enjoy your days off?"

I knew this was going to get ugly. Reg never called to chit-chat so I knew I was going to a scene.

"Yeah, the days off were good and I was thinking of calling you to see if I could have a couple more."

"We can talk about that later, but right now I have a case that I know you're going to enjoy."

"What case? The sun's just coming up and I'm still in sleep mode!"

"Okay, now listen up. Mike Smolenski is over on Lafayette and McDougal. He's got a naked male body, dumped in the street and burned to a crisp. If you're not too busy, do you think you could stop by and give him a hand?"

"Well, Reg, I was actually thinking about doing a little yard work today and maybe going down to see the Tigers play later on and . . . "

"Sure, Jackie. I'll let Mike know you're on the way."

Coleman A. Young, the mayor of Detroit, had earmarked the area of Lafayette and McDougal as crucial to the redevelopment of the Motor City. He hoped that it was going to be the crown jewel of his administration and had squeezed millions from wealthy suburbanites to insure its success. It was part of what was called urban renewal. The area had been heavily bulldozed, transients and bums moved, hookers jailed, and grass seeds and saplings spread around. Coincidentally, it was also the area where the mayor had been raised as a child.

Sergeant Mike Smolenski was at the scene, and was sitting in his car when I arrived. Mike was a seventeen-year veteran of the department and had spent the last two years at the Homicide Unit. He was quite proud of having attained a bachelor's degree in police science at Wayne State University and made sure that everyone knew about it. He really didn't like police work and by the time he had six years on the job he started to count the days till his retirement. He hated Detroit and dreamt of moving out of town to do private investigative work. With his lousy, negative attitude, I figured that he would make a decent investigator in divorce cases.

He had put in a rough night and had been to three previous homicide scenes. He was more than happy to have someone around who would appreciate his pain and labor. "What took you so long?"

"Well, Mike, I would have been here sooner but I decided to get dressed before leaving the house."

"Well, you could at least have worn something that matched. I'm glad this is your case and not mine. We got nothin' here. Only witnesses are the couple in the car who almost ran the body over. Luckily they saw the carcass in the street or it would be more screwed up than it already is. Whoever set him on fire only did half the job. You'd think if you were going to cook someone you'd at least go all the way. No barbeque sauce, nothing."

Mike had spent too much time in the streets and his gallows humor missed its mark.

Lying there in the street was the naked body of a black male, twenty to thirty years of age, curled into a half-circle position. He had suffered what appeared to be a shotgun wound going downward from his right shoulder traveling, at what looked like, a forty-five degree angle into his chest cavity. Someone had tried to incinerate the poor man and there was heavy charring around his head, shoulders, arms and hands. It was a very strange site and there were questions as to the accelerant used and the location of the crime. The nearest home was over one-hundred yards away and the majority of the dwellings had been demolished. There was no use in taking a survey and that pleased Mike. There were no witnesses, no identity, and not much to go on. This was not just a *whodunit,* it was, more importantly, a *whowasit.* Since there were no scorching signs or fibers at the scene, it was evident that he had been murdered, torched somewhere else and dumped in the street. I put my flashlight near his nose and didn't see any signs of smoke inhalation.

The evidence technicians arrived and I had them take photos and measurements and afterwards I released the scene to them. I drove the few miles back to headquarters and arrived just after 8 a.m.

After slugging down a couple of cups of eight-hour-old coffee, I walked the four blocks to the Wayne County Medical Examiner's Office, a.k.a. the morgue. My victim was now wearing a toe tag that identified him as John Doe #337. The medical opinion was that he had died of gunshot wounds that had penetrated his right shoulder and entered into his body on a downward angle. As the bullets traveled, they pierced many vital organs in the area of the chest, traversing through the lungs, liver and a few less important interior organs. Eight separate pellets were recovered. They looked like double-aught buckshot and were later confirmed so by the lab folks at the firearms section.

His hands and fingers were so burned that our fingerprint technician was unable to get readable prints. While at the morgue I had his hands amputated and sent to the Michigan State Police Laboratory in Lansing. It would be hours before I would know if the state people were successful in getting prints.

Finally, at 3:30 p.m., I received a call from Corporal Barry Cohn of the Michigan State Police. He related that he had been able to get some readable prints from the fingers and was faxing them to our Identification Unit. It was two hours later when I was notified that a match had been made with the identity of John Doe #337. The prints belonged to Roushell Worthy.

I walked down to the Identification Section and pulled the file on Roushell Worthy. He had been arrested four times for minor offenses. He was a thirty-two-year-old man and had given several different addresses for his home. He moved around quite a bit. So my friend and partner, Cal Noles, and I went looking for Roushell's residence and, hopefully, someone who cared about him. It was now just after 7 p.m. and we both were getting tired. Waiting around can cause that.

Cal had been my partner for just over three years. He was a few years older than me, measured out at 6'2" with a weight in excess of 240 pounds. He looked big and tough, but of the two of us he was the softest. He was ambitious and took his work seriously.

He had a difficult time speaking English without tossing in several cuss words. After a while, it was just part of him being him and it didn't bother me. He and his wife had three boys and they matched with the ages of my children. He and his clan had purchased a cottage in the Farwell area and lived within a mile of our place up north. Working with him was always enjoyable and having his family near ours in Farwell added to our times together.

The first two addresses that were checked were now vacant lots. The third stop took us to a single family dwelling on LaSalle Boulevard. The house was dark as we went to the door. The area had once been an area of wealth but was now one of poverty. Many homes were abandoned and plywood covered many windows. Of course, there was no doorbell. The door was secured with an iron grate, as were the windows.

Cal, who was never at a loss for words, mumbled, "This place is more secure than Jackson Prison."

Cal reached through the bars and pounded on the door with his Kell-Lite flashlight, leaving several indentations in the wood. An older gentleman appeared in a few seconds and after a brief conversation convinced us that Roushell had never lived there. We apologized for the intrusion and the man said, "We're used to being woke up around here, but usually it's by gunshots. This neighborhood is really goin' down."

It seemed to me that the neighborhood had been in demise for the last twenty years. I looked up and down the street and sadly realized that the vacant lots outnumbered the standing dwellings.

With that, we left. Cal was riding shotgun and within a mile he was asleep. My eyes were beginning to burn, my stomach was on fire from too much coffee, and I was starving. It was now 10:30 p.m. and Sunday morning was quickly approaching. There were few restaurants worth visiting at that time of night so I took the long route to Lyle's Restaurant on Michigan Avenue. It was in the suburb of Dearborn and was one of the few places open twenty-four hours a day. It was famous for ham sandwiches and bean soup. It was also Cal's favorite haunt.

I ran over a couple of curbs trying to awaken Cal, but it was useless. He was out. So I finally pulled into Lyle's lot and shook him a few times. I was just about ready to hit him with a couple of sprays of mace when he farted and came back to consciousness. The air that he expelled could have lifted the roof off of the Pontiac Silverdome Stadium. After hurling a couple of expletives at me, he complimented my driving and choice of eateries.

After dining we decided to continue our hunt. It was a wonder what energy came from bean soup and a ham sandwich. Cal asked me if I wanted him to drive and I quickly said, "Do you think I'm crazy?"

He grunted, and in a few words questioned my intelligence and the legitimacy of my birth, closed his eyes, and soon was, again, in the twilight zone.

It was just after midnight when we arrived at a lovely place called the Brewster Douglas Projects. There were twelve towers, each fourteen floors high. It was the first low-cost housing project built in Detroit and it was now the most decayed. Cal had once suggested that we erect a sign and title this place *Despairsville.* In the daylight the place could be frightening; at night it could be intimidating and downright dangerous. It was of small comfort to me that Cal hadn't qualified with his pistol in over eight years.

We took the stairs up four flights to a unit with the address 448. It, too, had been one of Roushell's former addresses. We knocked on the door and after several minutes an elderly lady opened it. We identified ourselves, which was hardly necessary, and the lady who was wrapped in a long housecoat told us her name was Icy Mae Russell.

"Mrs. Russell, do you know Roushell Worthy?"

"Why, yes, he's my grandson. Has he done somethin'?"

"No, ma'am. We are just trying to find where he last lived. Does he live here?"

"No, he's been at his momma's house. She's my daughter."

"Can you give us her address?"

"Why, yes, I mean I don't rightly know, but it's up on McClellan, on the east side of Detroit, you know."

"Do you know the cross street?"

"Why, yes, it's down from Canfield. They live in a nice house with some blue trim. The house is mostly white. Do you gentlemens want some coffee or some water or anything?"

I was afraid that Cameron was going to say, "Why, yes," so I said, "No, thanks Mrs. Russell, we got to be goin'. Do you have the phone number of your daughter?"

"Why, no. I don't even have a phone."

When I looked at her worn pieces of furniture it was easy to believe that she didn't own a phone. The poor dear must have ranked in the lower level of the poverty scale. As we were leaving, my hard-nosed partner pulled a five out of his wallet and left it on the table.

We left and headed to the east side of Detroit.

It was just after 1 a.m. when we turned off of McClellan and found a small white house with blue trim. All the lights were off as we rang the doorbell. After a few minutes, a young female opened the door.

"Sorry to wake you, we're from the police department and we're trying to locate the home of Roushell Worthy. Is this his home?"

"Um hum."

Her eyes were half-closed. She didn't seem the least bit nervous and was either still very much asleep or somewhat retarded. We learned soon that she was very slow.

"May we come in?"

"Um hum."

"Do you know Roushell Worthy?"

"Um hum, he's my brother."

"And your name?"

"Cynthia Worthy."

A voice of a woman came from the bedroom just to our right. "Who's that, Cynthia?"

Cynthia answered, "It's the police."

I walked over to the bedroom entrance and said, "Hi, I'm Sergeant Loshaw from the police department."

Lying in the bed was a heavyset woman of about fifty. The bed was a hospital bed, complete with side-rails. She had an intravenous tube connected to her forearm.

She had a concerned look and said, "What do you want Roushell for?"

It wasn't going to be easy telling her that he was dead. "Are you related to Roushell?"

"Why, yes, He's my son."

"When did you last see him?"

"I know he was here Friday night. He's not in trouble is he?"

"When he was here Friday, did anything unusual happen that night?"

I noticed that Cynthia was moving from foot to foot. Her eyes were darting from ceiling to floor and beads of perspiration were forming on her forehead.

"Why, yes. It was really strange because Moses lit off a bunch of firecrackers or somethin' that made a bunch of noise."

"Who is Moses?"

"That's Cynthia's boyfriend. Moses Bates."

"Did anything else unusual take place?"

"Why, yes. After them crackers went off, the house got real smoky. I yelled at them two boys to open some windows and to stop the messin' around. I'm sick and can't get outta the bed and they be fussin' and almost settin' fire to the house."

Cynthia was really swaying now.

"What's your first name, Mrs. Worthy?"

"It's Gladys and I'm on full disability."

"Can we have your permission to look around your house?"

"Why, sure. We ain't done nothin' and ain't got nothin' to hide."

Cal and I began to look around. It didn't take long and we knew we had found our murder scene. On the wall by the stairs leading to an upstairs bedroom was what looked like smeared blood. A very weak attempt had been made to clean the area. There were some dark spots in the carpeting on the stairs. The area was still damp.

Tears were beginning to form in Cynthia's eyes.

"Cynthia, is your boyfriend upstairs?"

"No, he went to his other girlfriend's place."

"Oh, and where's that?"

"I dunno. She stays over on Van Dyke and Harper."

"You know the street?"

"I think it's Knodell."

"What's her name?"

"Missy. She's got two babies by Moses."

"Cynthia, do you have any recent pictures of Moses, or of you and Moses?"

With that, she went to her room and came back with her purse. She took out her wallet. Inside was a four-picture strip of her and Moses that she had taken when they were shopping at Kresge's.
Ol' Moses was a handsome looking guy, complete with Gerri-curls and a missing upper front tooth. I was sure that the picture didn't do him justice.

We continued our search through the house. In the basement was an old conversion-type furnace with the tubular vents. The furnace door, a hinged 12" by 14" affair was ajar and there were obvious signs of flesh sticking to the metal entrance. We eventually took our search outside the house where we found a trail of blood and burned flesh leading down a sidewalk toward the alley.

We called for evidence technicians and had them take photographs, draw sketches, and collect samples of the suspected flesh and blood.

We told Gladys that we were going to convey her daughter Cynthia down to our office for an "official statement" and then we would bring her back. Gladys made a few phone calls and assured us that she had some friends coming over to take care of her.

Once we arrived at Homicide I decided to have a technician video tape my interview with Cynthia. I wanted to show proof that she wasn't mistreated and that she had enough basic reasoning ability to give a truthful account of what had occurred. I also wanted to protect the investigation in case she somehow developed amnesia or got herself killed.

To be on the safe side, I advised her of her constitutional rights. I even had her read the first two sentences, which she did hesitatingly, so that I knew she could read. She gave a very thorough account of the murder. There had been bad blood between Moses and Roushell for some time. Apparently, Roushell objected to Moses slapping his little sister around. Moses had been staying in the upper bedroom of the bungalow and kept a twelve gauge shotgun near his bed. He told the family that it was just there in case they ever needed protection. Moses and Roushell had an argument about some missing weed. Moses raced up the stairs, grabbed the gun, and fired one shot from the banister as Roushell was starting up the stairs. That cleared up the mystery of the strange entry wound.

Moses, being the bright man that he was, then tried to burn the body by forcing a portion of it through the door of the furnace. Of course, he was only partially successful. At one point he realized that the furnace only had a pilot light going, so he ran upstairs and jacked the thermostat up to ninety degrees and heard the furnace ignite. In a short time, the flesh began to burn and smoke started to fill the house. All the time Cynthia was at his side.

At some point he came to the conclusion that this was not going to work, so he pulled the body out of the furnace grate, carried it up the stairs, and outside to the alley. He drove his car around to the back, put the body in the trunk, and drove away.

After the interview, we placed the tape on evidence, updated the teletype, and had Cynthia driven back home. It was now approaching 5 a.m. I walked into an empty interrogation room, clicked off the light, sat down, and closed my eyes. Once Cal saw that the interrogation of Cynthia was going as planned, he had retired to the Women's Detention area where he found a bed with all the fixings. Cal was much smarter than I.

After a short nap, I woke my partner and we decided to drive over to the east side. The sun was making its appearance and its rays were burning our eyes. Cal settled that by closing his and in a few minutes was sawing logs again. It was at least seven hours after his bedtime and he looked like he had just gone twelve rounds with Mohammad Ali. Actually, on his very best days, he looked like he had gone six rounds with the Champ. After hitting a couple of potholes and curbs, he opened his eyes and said, "Well, I think it's about time we started earning the big money that the City's paying us."

He was primed and ready to go. With that, we turned off of Van Dyke and headed in the direction of Knodell Street. It was a short street that went on for only three blocks and, to our good fortune, a newsboy was delivering the

Detroit Free Press. Cal motioned him over to our car, showed him the picture of Moses, and asked if he delivered to a woman named Missy. He gave us the address and we were in business. The house was on the third block. We cruised by and parked the car four houses south of the dwelling. We called for a uniform backup and when they arrived we sent them to the rear of the house.

Cal and I walked up the stairs and knocked on the door. A young lady came to the door with her finger to her lips and gave us the "shhhh" sound. She must have known we were coming and said, "He's in the basement."

"Moses? Does he have a gun?"

"I dunno. I'm scared of him. He's so mean."

"Is anyone else in the house?"

"No, my momma took the babies."

"Okay. You go across the street or sit in our car."

Cal and I made our way into the house and checked it out. There was no one on the main floor. The house was a ramshackle mess that looked like it had been recently burglarized. We opened the back door and the uniformed men came in. We yelled out that we were police officers and heard movement coming from the basement. I turned on the light switch and announced that we were coming down. As I began creeping down the stairs I became painfully aware of how inadequate my little Colt Cobra felt in my hand. Six shots, two and a half inch barrel, six ounces—not much of a security blanket. My heart was pounding harder than usual. What was going on? I had made a lot of arrests, why was this one taking a toll? Premonition? I didn't believe in that. Why was I doing this? You're going to get yourself killed. For what? I guess I liked being a hero. No, I think a shrink would say that I was still trying to get my father's approval. As a cop I certainly realized that there were times when I was fearful, but unlike normal people, I had little choice in the matter. This was a combination of fear and honor that I didn't have time to figure out. I was physically pretty well empty and I allowed myself to believe that my anxiety was because of tiredness. In a few seconds it would all be over with.

As I hit the bottom of the stairs I saw Moses sitting on a lawn chair with a shotgun lying on the floor at his feet. I yelled, "Don't move an inch or you're dead."

I half expected him to reach for the gun, that way forcing me to shoot him and saving him from committing suicide. He just sat there and started laughing. We ran to him, stood him up, and cuffed him. He then started crying. To say the least, he was sending out some mixed messages.

We walked him out of the house and conveyed him to homicide. After advising him of his constitutional rights, he gave me a fairly truthful account of the shooting. One of the strangest parts of the confession had to do with Moses driving around town for over four hours with Roushell Wothy's dead, burned body in the trunk of his car. He even stopped to eat at a cheap diner on 12th street. While cruising around he was stopped for a driving infraction. He had enough presence of mind, and a bit of swagger, to talk himself out of a ticket. That may have been one of his proudest moments. During the interrogation we built quite a bond and he reluctantly told me that he had a brother who was a Detroit Police Officer. When it was over it was just past 9 a.m.

Our squad boss, Reg Hart, walked up to us, "Jack, you and Cal look like you could use some sleep. You guys go home, say hi to your families and come back in a few hours."

"Boss, that sounds like a good idea."

"We'll make sure that Moses doesn't go anywhere. By the way, you and Cal did some nice work here today and there's no sense in both of you coming in to finish the paperwork right away. Heck, I know that Cal can't type, so you might as well come in, let's say by two, and you can type out the warrant request."

"You paying me overtime?"

"Now wait a minute, you know we always bank your overtime. Plus, I know how much you love to spend the extra hours at your cottage."

"You are some sweet-talker . . . but I'd rather have the overtime."

"We'll think about that."

On my way home, I took a detour and went over to the Worthy house on McClellan Street. I awoke Cynthia and her mother and told them of the events. They both cried, one having lost a son, and the other losing a brother and a boyfriend. However, they looked relieved and somehow managed to thank me.

I got in my city Plymouth and drove home.

It was Sunday morning, a little after ten, when I pulled into the driveway. I got out of the car and headed for the back of the house. For some unknown reason all the Loshaws entered the house through the family room door. I opened the gate and walked over to the pool. The hum of the filter and smell of chlorine were alive and it helped bring me back to reality. I had been out chasing Moses Bates that night and my wife and kids were in church.

It was quite a contrast. They were in church and would never know what it was like in that murky pool of "dog-eat-dog" mentality that was outside of their worlds.

I went into the house and crept up the stairs. I felt very tired and alone. There were times when I wanted to tell Pat how scared I was, but I never did. There were times I wanted to do something that was "clean" but couldn't. This was my call, this was what I was supposed to do, and I did it. But there were times when it was lonely.

I put the handcuffs through the Cobra's cylinder and put the weapon in my sock drawer. I threw my shirt in the hamper, tie on a hanger, hung my pants on the top of the door and rolled into bed. After pounding the pillow for a few minutes, I was gone.

I awoke at 1 p.m., brushed my teeth and prepared to go back downtown.

"Hi Honey. Did you catch any bad guys?"

"Yeah, a bunch of 'em. How was church?

"Good. The kids are in the pool. It's hot enough. Wanna talk?"

"Nah, it'll just get me wound up. I have to go in to finish some paperwork. I should be home in a couple of hours. Reg owes me so I don't think I'll be late."

***

Monday morning came around and when I heard the children getting ready for school I climbed out of bed. I wasn't a detective to them, nor hero, nor solver of great mysteries . . . just dad. They treated me just that way. No fuss, no muss, just in a hurry to get out the door and contend with the issues of their young lives. Being their dad was the best job I've ever had. Pat loaded them up in our trusty '76 Ford van and off they went.

On the trip down Gratiot I kept thinking about Moses' brother the cop. How was he going to react? How was he feeling? Would he come to hate me as Moses certainly would? What would it be like for Moses, the brother of a policeman, to spend the rest of his life in prison? Would he pay a further price for his brother being a cop?

The warrant request was simple and straightforward. I walked it over to the prosecutor's office and met with APA Rich Krissus. He quickly scanned the paperwork and asked what I thought of Murder Two. It was the correct charge. For the next twenty minutes we talked about all the major sports. He was a sports junkie, so we talked the Tigers. The Honorable David Cavanaugh signed the warrant request. He even asked about my family and how I was doing. I told him that everything was fine, but I was disturbed because Moses Bates was the brother of a Detroit Police Officer. The judge said, "Well, I guess that in some cases we truly can't be our brother's keeper."

165

I thanked him and suggested that we get together someday for lunch and he smiled and agreed. We both knew that it would never happen. Now it was simply a matter of waiting for the wheels of justice to roll. The case was Homicide File 82-335, the People vs. Moses Bates, assigned to the 36th District Court, housed in the Frank Murphy Hall of Justice.

As a purely historical note, Frank Murphy was a Recorder's Court judge in the 1920s and would become the Mayor of Detroit, then the Governor of Michigan, then U.S. Attorney General, and eventually a U.S. Supreme Court Justice.

The trial began on November 14, 1982. Moses's court appointed attorney was a veteran of the Murphy Hall of Justice named Bill Michaelson. On his best days he was a formidable opponent. Sadly, his best days were far behind him and the ones that remained were few and far between. In his former days he was known as a jury charmer, but now those old persuasive techniques were suddenly irritants to jurors. To his credit he recognized he was no Clarence Darrow and waived his clients' right to a jury trial, opting to allow the Honorable Henry Heaston to hear the case. It promised to be a speedy trial, as required by the Constitution.

Judge Heaston was an able jurist with a wonderful sense of humor. He reminded me of Sammy Davis Jr. playing "Here Comes the Judge" on the TV show *Laugh In*. Some of the judges notable one-liners, which he repeated often, were, "Do you mean to tell me that this occurred within the corporate limits of Detroit?"

And to a worried defendant who was posting bond: "Now let me tell you this, if you don't show up on your scheduled court appearance, you will be caught and incarcerated. You do know what incarceration means, don't you?"

Of course, the defendant had no idea as to the meaning, but readily agreed that he did.

The judge continued, "And I will put a bond on you so high that Henry Ford won't be able to get you out of jail."

And his favorite that he recited to every defendant, "If you ever come before me again, the only thing that will beat you to the State Prison in Southern Michigan will be the headlights on the bus."

He was a funny man who, despite his tough talk, in reality, was lenient when it came to sentencing.

The case was adjourned to the following morning. The prosecutor, named Wayne Garber, was a grizzled old veteran, who wouldn't consider a lesser charge plea. He could smell blood and wanted some. So, at 10 a.m., the trial started. There were a handful of witnesses and things moved swiftly. Four hours later Moses Bates was found guilty of Murder Two. The verdict was a surprise to all, not that he was guilty of anything less, but that the judge actually followed the law and found him guilty of what he was charged with. We were all expecting a Manslaughter verdict. Murder Two carried any term of years up to life and gave the judge great latitude in his sentencing decision. Mr. Bates almost passed out and his attorney looked shocked and frightened as he quickly threw the court papers in his briefcase and mumbled something about a miscarriage of justice and how an appeal would be soon in coming.

It was shortly after finishing this case that my friend, Cal Noles, began complaining of stomach pain. We went to our normal cop restaurants and Cal ate little. In Cal's usual manner, he would eat helpings of lunch to the point that I accused him of eating as though he was going to an execution in the morning. So, after two months of pain and complaining, he went to the doctor. The diagnosis wasn't good.

Chapter Twelve: The Story of Danny Rouse

It is not the critic who counts. The credit belongs to the man in the arena,
whose face is marred by dust and sweat and blood. Who strives valiantly and
who at the worst, if he fails, at least falls, while daring greatly. So that his
place shall never be with those cold and timid souls who neither have known
victory or defeat.
-- Teddy Roosevelt

As a boy growing up on the east side of Detroit in the 1950s, my very best friend was Billy Rouse. He and his family lived two doors away from my home. We played on the same baseball and basketball teams and had adjoining Detroit News paper routes. Bill and I enjoyed listening to new music called rock and roll especially on the radio dial of 1500 AM with the popular disc-jockey, Tom Clay. The music was considered rebellious in nature, especially by adults, and was loved by teenagers.

Billy Rouse and I were friends and saw each other every day. Danny was two years younger than his brother, Billy, and made himself a bother by trying to hang out with us older guys. He wasn't a bad kid, but he sure was a pest and a constant tagalong. Billy slept at my home quite often but his little brother was not allowed. Billy made it known to my mother that his brother wet the bed, so our home was off limits. Of course, Billy's story was untrue.

Billy was clearly the favored child of his father until a surprise package arrived in their home when Billy was fifteen. Her name was Jenny and she soon swept her father's heart. Danny, being the middle child and the least liked, seemed to be the most needy. I usually felt sorry for him but I had similar issues at home, so I kept my feelings to myself.

Mr. Rouse liked to drink and, on occasion, showed his wife, Arlene, that he was the boss by smacking her around. All the neighbors knew about it, but in those days people overlooked such things and referred to them as "family situations." It was believed that if ignored long enough these situations would simply disappear.

Mr. Rouse was proud of his nickname, "Hit-and-Run Bill." He had worked at the old Dodge main plant in Hamtramck, which was only three miles from his home. Each night after work he made it a point to stop at his favorite three saloons. His concoction of choice was something commonly known as a boilermaker. It consisted of a shell of beer and a shot of cheap bar whiskey. Being a man of temperance, he only allowed himself three of these combinations at each tavern. After finishing a combination, he would then run to his next stop.

By the time Mr. Rouse arrived home he would be sufficiently drunk to endure the cold indifference of his spouse. He never admitted that he had drunk too much because it had become well known that he could hold his liquor.

Young Danny had learned that it was wise to avoid his father when he arrived home from work. He knew that even though his report card was better than Billy's, and even though he was faithful in mowing the lawn, and even though he kept his room clean, it was smarter to not breathe the same air as his dad upon his arrival.

Mr. Rouse always had the time to seek Danny out and managed to belittle and criticize him. There weren't many things about Danny that pleased his father.

Billy was a different story. He had learned to gain his father's approval by treating Danny as though he was a leper. I'm sorry to say that in order to keep Billy in his father's favor, there were times when I was mean to Danny too. I have deep regrets about that. It was something that was pushed out of my mind and never talked about.

In my senior year at Northeastern High School my family moved out of Detroit to the suburb of Center Line. Center Line had the distinction of being the first Michigan city to have a white line painted on the highway separating traffic, thus its name. The town was only two miles outside of the Eight Mile Road boundary of Detroit. Even though it was a short distance between the two cities, with my family's move, I lost track of the Rouse family and I went on with my life.

In February 1983, I was at a murder scene where a baseball cap was found twenty feet from the victim's body. The victim had died from multiple stab wounds and there were several defensive wounds to his hands that indicated a struggle. I called for a canine unit to respond to the scene, and to my surprise, the police officer who arrived was Danny Rouse with his German shepherd, Pokey.

Danny had grown to be a tall, muscular, good-looking man with six years of police experience. Somehow, he recognized me and walked over with his hand out and said, "Hi, Jack. I'm your old neighbor, Danny. Is it alright if I call you Jack?"

"No problem, Danny. How long have you been a cop?"

"Just over six years and now I'm doing what I love. You need to say "hi" to Pokey. He's the best partner in the world."

I petted his dog and told him about the cap and watched the two of them as they worked. It was a thrill to see this once snot-nosed annoyance now in a blue uniform . . . all grown up and looking like a man.

I was thoroughly impressed with Danny's handling of the evidence and his dog. Within moments Pokey had picked up the scent and led us to a nearby vacant house where our suspect was found hiding in the basement. The suspect looked terrified as the one-hundred and forty pound dog began barking and clawing toward him.

After closing the scene we all travelled back to 1300 Beaubien, Police Headquarters. Once I had finished interrogating the prisoner, I had a chance to sit down and talk with Danny. He was now thirty-seven years old, married, and the father of two daughters. He told me that his mother had died and his dad had remarried. He quickly acknowledged that he and his father had little to no relationship. He also went on to tell me that Billy and he seldom spoke.

He said he had seen my name in the papers a few times, but wasn't sure if he should have contacted me. He told me that he thought it was "cool" that I had made it to homicide.

I told Danny that I thought it was "cool" the way he and Pokey had tracked the killer down and we were both smiling and having fun.

Danny reached down, petted Pokey, and said, "I told my wife that it was good that someone from the old neighborhood had made it all the way to homicide. I was gonna call you a couple of times but I wasn't sure you'd remember me."

I thought his expectations of success were fairly low, but in the same breath it was gratifying that he viewed me as someone he respected. At that point I had an aching feeling that caused me to wish I had been nicer to him as we were growing up. I know that life isn't always fair and I hurt for Danny's childhood situation. I was certainly pleased about his marriage and the daughters in his life.

As we talked I noticed a very faint odor of alcohol coming from Danny. I shrugged it off and assumed it was my imagination.

He turned in his reports and we gave each other manly hugs. We promised to stay in touch . . . promises that we knew we likely wouldn't keep.

* * *

At the time I came across Danny Rouse and his canine partner Pokey, I was assigned to an eight man unit called the Special Assignment Squad. Originally it was thought that its name would be the Police Investigative Shooting Squad, or the Special Homicide Investigative Team. A quick look at the acronyms caused those suggestions to be scrapped and S.A.S. became the title. We were responsible for the investigation of cases deemed "high profile" . . . which meant those that were newsworthy and any cases where police officers were involved in homicides.

Six months had passed since I had met with Danny. I had just finished my summer furlough, or vacation in civilian language, when I returned to work to find that our squad had picked up three new cases in my absence. Two of the cases had been closed and the third was soon to be finalized. After going through the case files, I began reading some of the other reports.

I pulled out the most recent, a suicide file, and read the outside jacket. I stared at the name and my heart began to pound. *"Danny Rouse—Suicide 83-088—death by self-inflicted gunshot wound."* I could feel the blood pounding through my temples and my eyes began to water.

Without thinking I opened the file and went to the crime scene photos. I pulled out the first photo and there was Danny, this good looking kid from the old neighborhood, lying on his side on a dirty oil-stained cement garage floor. In his right hand was a .357 Magnum revolver and there were clear signs of an ugly exit wound to his head. His black hair was caked with blood.

There were several other photographs of the scene, but the one I had in my hand was enough for me. I put it back in the file with the others.

I sat there for a few moments trying to make sense of it all. I felt helpless and very lonely. I thought to myself, "Why did you have to look at the photo? Do you always have to be the homicide cop? What's the matter with you?"

My squad lieutenant, Reg Hart, walked over to me. "Jack, is everything okay? Did you know Rouse?"

It took me a moment to answer, "Yeah, boss. We grew up together. Any idea why he did it?"

"Jack, you know what happens when people get down, and he was pretty drunk at the time. Man, I'm really sorry. Suicide is a b----!"

I excused myself and walked over to the men's bathroom. I put my back to the door and tears welled up. As I stood there, I told myself that I had to get things together. I turned the cold water on and splashed my face. I looked into the mirror and didn't like the guilt that I saw. I posed a question. "Why didn't you call him like you said you would? You could have stopped this. He looked up to you. You call yourself a *detective* and you weren't smart enough to *detect* that he had a problem."

I cried some real tears for a minute and asked God to forgive me. I stood there questioning the sincerity of my "faith-walk" and my ability to help others. I promised God that I would not let another opportunity to make a difference slip through my hands like this one had.

Finally, I felt sufficiently together to walk back into the world of my peers. I returned to the suicide file, avoided the pictures, and pulled out the morgue protocol. It showed that Rouse had a blood alcohol content of .22, well over the .07 limit to be declared too drunk to drive.

I looked into some of the miscellany reports which showed Rouse had been sent for counseling regarding his drinking problem. I feared the sins of the father had visited him.

I have always viewed suicides as being selfish and cruel. Suicides hurt all those who cared about the victim. He left behind a young wife and two little girls . . . and a hole in my heart.

Chapter Thirteen: When I Left Homicide

One of my partners and closest friend was a man named Cal Noles. Cal was one of those big guys who was as soft as a Teddy Bear. He was the fastest speaker I had ever heard. His words would often jumble together and during times of excitement he spoke with such velocity that he was unintelligible. When on the byways of the Motor City, talking to street-people, his nerves often became frayed and he would be asked to repeat himself. That made things worse and he would look at me and say, "Would you try to explain to this jerk what I just said?"

And just to add some fuel to the fire I retorted, "I'd be glad to Cal, but I didn't understand you either."

With that, he would begin sputtering a multitude of words that I often suspected were swear words, but thankfully they were unintelligible, too.

He had a gruff exterior, but his heart was as soft as melted ice cream. Many times I saw him reach in his pocket to give money to homeless folks, or as they were called in police circles "Jakey bums." I heard him say, "I know they will probably spend it on dope or booze, but it bugs me to just walk by them."

"Well, Cal, if you're just gonna give your money away, give it to me and I promise not to spend it on dope."

Cal spit out a few profanities and said, "It's my money and I'll do what I want."

During the four years we worked together, we always managed to sneak over to Tiger Stadium on opening day and watch an inning or two of the game. We felt like teenagers skipping school as we stood in the aisle cheering our home town heroes. I loved working with him and knew that my backside was always covered. He often said of his wife, Elaine, who had emigrated from Ireland to the United States, that she was so poor they had her thirteen floors below deck hanging out with the potatoes. Cal and Elaine had three sons that matched up well with my kids. We enjoyed working together so much that we bought a cottage in Farwell, Michigan, a mile apart from each other. Our wives and children got along well and Cal and I enjoyed drowning worms and telling war stories.

In May of 1982, Cal began complaining of stomach pain. He loved chili and hot dogs and often swallowed them down with two cans of Pepsi. His stomach burned after each meal and finally he went to a doctor. After a few tests he underwent surgery and cancer was found. Four months later, in September of 1982, he died.

The day after he died, I was working by myself. I felt a bit aimless without him. I was driving my unmarked, department-owned Plymouth on Michigan Avenue. As I approached Michigan and Trumbull, the site of Tiger Stadium, I began thinking about the times we spent at the park and my eyes welled with tears. I missed my old friend. My vision became so blurred that I had to pull the car to the curb. After a time, I collected myself and continued my drive back to headquarters.

As I thought about Cal and some other friends of mine that had died, I realized that there were times, as a homicide detective, when I felt very alone. I had a wife and four children and I didn't want them to know of the risks I took, or the challenges, or the blood, or the decaying bodies. Of all the detectives I worked with, I wasn't sure how many felt the weight of solving cases the way I did. There were only a few who seemed to share some of my passion; Cal was one of those, and now he was gone.

As I have looked back at my career, the thing that I missed most was the camaraderie. There was a unique bonding that took place between the people who gave their all to work at Homicide. We felt that we were special, we were the elite, and it was as if we had a secret handshake that was known only to those of us who understood and appreciated the privilege.

We were a group of people who shared in the challenges, the hunt, the chase, and the dangers. Oh, there were times of irreverent laughter and often there were secret sobs. The unit, it seemed, was for those who really cared, the called . . . the ordained. It required a certain amount of intelligence, generous doses of confidence, a fair amount of moxie, and street smarts. Chutzpah helped too. And it didn't hurt to have optimism and a strong belief in right and wrong.

Those of us at Homicide worked for the City of Detroit; at least that's what the paychecks indicated. Yet, we knew that we worked for each other. Each case was a challenge to our pride . . . pride as an individual and pride in knowing that every case could be solved. We often felt like private contractors, hired by the municipality. We were team members who trusted and relied on each other. We took great pride in our accomplishments and it meant more when greeted with handshakes, pats on the back, and words of praise from the select few who understood. When an impossible case was solved there was electricity, a glow and a high that addicts would never know. When those seemingly impossible cases were completed it caused flashes of wonder in the outsider, envy in those less gifted, and a new sense of purpose for those who cared.

Many homicide detectives were unusual people. To the irritation of many wives, most enjoyed being around their comrades more than with members of their households. Sadly, many wives were known to feel excluded and jealousy was a common companion. Divorce was common; alcohol was a mocking clown and suicide an enticing option.

It was not uncommon for us to work around the clock on a case. And when the mission was accomplished, it was normal to relax only when in the company of those who understood. It was there, where the conversations were about the bloody business that we had chosen, that the true bonds of brotherhood were forged. It was as if we could only relax when with those of like spirit.

We lived in a real world that often seemed a fantasy. It was about climbing mountains, rescuing damsels, righting wrongs, and untying the Gordian knot. In many ways we were still little boys playing cops and robbers . . . but now with real guns, and real blood and real death.

It seemed to me that many detectives spent large amounts of time and energy talking about retirement. It was dreamed about and eagerly anticipated . . . and it was a cruel joke. After a life of facing challenges, how could we be thrust into a world that seemed to have little purpose? Who could make sense of a world with no enemy to conquer? Imagine a world without a Goliath breathing his threats and curses . . . and to think there would be no David to say, "Is there not a cause?" No armor to put on, no windmills to attack . . .

Sir Winston Churchill, the great British statesman, once said, "There is no greater feeling in this world than to be shot at without effect."

I have great respect for Sir Winston, but cannot agree. The greatest feeling that I have felt is when right overcomes evil . . . and I have lived to see it many times. I cannot go through life without remembering that it is He, who hides an oak tree in a little acorn, and that causes me to know that truth does win out.

With those thoughts in mind, I decided it was time for me to leave the Homicide Unit. It was a wonderful experience that lasted over nine years. I worked with some of the finest people I had ever met and I knew I would miss them, but it was time to leave, and I did.

My next adventure wasn't nearly as risky as working the streets of Detroit, but it too was a faith journey. And that story will soon be written.

Jack Loshaw

CPSIA information can be obtained at www.ICGtesting.com
Printed in the USA
LVOW11s1737030814

397249LV00001B/8/P